Praise for *Get Your Brag On! Business Edition*

I was not yet 29 years old when the book, It's Time to Brag! *and Jeannette's keynote presentation,* Get Your Brag On! *truly changed my business and positively influenced my life, and the lives of others. I've been a guest speaker for several universities in marketing and business courses and Jeannette's ears must have been ringing. The book changed how I talked about and shared myself. It propelled my business to the next level not only locally, but regionally and nationally, including doing choreographic work on Broadway!*

Truly, thank you, Jeannette for doing what you are doing for it matters and it's influencing and changing lives for the better!

—Kayleigh Schadwinkel-Hickman
Owner/Dance Entrepreneur/Traveling Choreographer
POYDS Dance Company and KASH Dance & Choreography

I initially thought the Brag *work was nonsense. How wrong I was! Jeannette's techniques have profoundly reshaped how I approach goals, milestones, and achievements. The transformation I've experienced is undeniable. The results speak for themselves—just give the book a read and see the difference for yourself.*

—Jason Burnett
Director, Sales Enablement
Coach Financing

I've known Jeannette for many years and know the difference her books have made for me and for my clients.

Get Your Brag On! is a book I've been recommending to my coaching clients, many of whom need help improving their sales and management results. The problem was, they weren't able to define why people should work with them. After completing the exercises in the book, they were able to clearly and powerfully define the value they provide and Jeannette's book increased their confidence too.

—Diane Putvin
Business Partner & Coach
DL Consulting, LLC

Get Your Brag On! *gave me the chance to tell my business story without feeling like I was trying to be clever, like most marketing plans seem to emphasize. I found out that when Bragging I am speaking my truth and not someone else's twist on it. What an incredible difference it has made for me in all my business interactions!*

—Peggy Sue Schmoldt, Consultant
Educator and Keynote Speaker for the Beauty Industry
Founder and Owner of the Academy of Cosmetology Arts

Jeannette taught me that learning how to appropriately brag and own up to my own accomplishments helped me gain new clients, and realize I wasn't just an assistant, but a consultant and marketing strategist.

—Bobby Crew
Author of the Bestselling Book, *Dining with Devils*,
and Founder of The Horror Crew Productions
Publishing and Book Marketing Consultant

Jeannette Seibly's advice to brag quantifiably pays off! I have used the steps she discusses in Get Your Brag On! *I got new clients and won awards. The steps worked for me and they will work for you.*

—Jill S. Tietjen, P.E.
President and CEO
Technically Speaking

When it comes to teaching businesspeople to Get Your Brag On!, Jeannette Seibly is THE expert. Jeannette understands how selling yourself is what business growth is all about. If you are looking for the "win," then you need to feel comfortable and confident praising your abilities. Get Your Brag On! is a must-read for entrepreneurs, business owners, employees and job hunters alike.

—Andrea Pass, Owner
Andrea Pass Public Relations

Jeannette is truly one of a kind. She and I have been friends for a while and I am a huge fan of her book! She teaches you how to easily tell people what you do, why you are good at what you do, why people should work with you, and what they could get from working with you. This book has allowed our company to attract more new clients than any approach we have ever used. The best part is you never sound like a "braggard", you never sound salesy, and you are making it easy for prospective clients to feel comfortable with you. I highly recommend you read Jeannette's book and Get Your Brag On!

—Scott Lask
Scott Lask Wealth Management Group LLC
Founder and Managing Director

How exciting to find Get Your Brag On! and then to discover that it's not that difficult to implement the recommended process. Jeannette gives us five definitive steps to follow. Her approach will be eye-opening for many and affirming for others. Yet, it feels so logical and comfortable. After you read the book and do the exercises like I did, you will find it easy to incorporate bragging to get the right job or attract new clients. And, she makes it kind of fun.

—Karen Ross, Performance Mindset Expert

Business Edition

GET YOUR BRAG ON!

Sell Yourself and Win in Five Easy Steps

Jeannette L. Seibly

Get Your Brag On! Sell Yourself and Win in Five Easy Steps
Business Edition

Published by

MOUNTAIN
OWL
PRESS

Editor: Jill S. Tietjen, Technically Speaking
Cover and Interior Design: Nick Zelinger, NZGraphics.com
eBook Interior: Rebecca Finkel, F+P Design

ISBN: 979-8-9913639-0-7 (print)
ISBN: 979-8-9913639-1-4 (eBook)
LCCN: 2024918871

Get Your Brag On! includes updated brag information from earlier books and new information on negotiation, pitching, and sharing your ideas using your brags.

Printed in the United States of America

CONTENTS

Note from Jeannette …

"In praise of bragging …"[1] I read this headline in *The Wall Street Journal* and applauded!

After more than 30 years of sharing with people how to be present and share their accomplishments to win a sale, job, or contract; celebrate their wins; and share these feats; I could finally say to the people who have been dismissing the importance of bragging, "I told you so!"

Why is this so important to me?

I've seen so many women (and men) play small, dummy-down their successes (even when it was a new job opportunity or sale they really wanted and were qualified for), and avoid deserved recognition.

During a period of unemployment, I created the KTAs (Steps One through Three in this book) and shared them with other job seekers, from hourly employees to executives. They were excited to finally have a structure to help guide them in documenting their achievements. The KTAs helped them feel confident in providing a method of sharing their achievements and winning the job offer.

Then, I noticed, as a member of the National Association of Women Business Owners (NAWBO)—Detroit, Michigan Chapter, that many women were not receiving contracts that they were well-qualified to fulfill. I also noticed as a new business owner (more than 30 years ago—nothing has changed) that many women accepted less money and less opportunities than their skills merited. After I worked with one woman, a new business owner, she won the contract

---

[1] Robson, David, "In praise of bragging", *The Wall Street Journal*, https://www.wsj.com/lifestyle/relationships/in-praise-of-bragging-f726b125, June 20, 2024.

and her business revenues grew. It came from sharing her accomplishments in a way that could be received well and painted the right and best picture for her.

Lastly, when I was nominated for the NAWBO Leadership Award, the women that were encouraging me (and rewriting) my bio kept asking for more specifics. (Yes, I won.)

That's when the light went on!

After those experiences, I designed the structure to help everyone create their "KTAs," "I am …," and "My background includes …" I love watching the light go on for others and seeing them get the business, clients, new jobs, and awards they deserve. I want to share my method with everyone!

Everyone has accomplished a lot in their lives. But we often fail to own our wins for many reasons. Today, more than ever, it's time for each of us to stand up, speak up, and recognize and appreciate our many achievements.

Sharing your successes and wins effectively isn't hard. But it does require clarity about what you've accomplished. Many of you are not even aware of your own "wins."

Too often, you will:

- Rely on and hope others will do it for you. (Hint: They are not present to *their* own accomplishments. It's unreasonable to rely on them to want to know or wish to share *your* achievements.)

- Find people who are jealous of you or in denial that you can make a positive difference when they don't feel they've been able to do so or are still dreaming and hoping to achieve the same or similar results someday.

- Feel exhausted attempting to plug away at doing the "same old same old," hoping the next networking meeting, one-on-one meeting, sales presentation, or RFP/RFQ (Request for Proposal/Request for Quotation) will produce better results. Abracadabra rarely occurs if you're not in action sharing your successes in a business-savvy manner.

Sadly, while we wait for that perfect time, we:

- Lose recognition and clients when we don't step up to share our successes—people are not mind readers.

- Fail to obtain awards for government or company contracts when we underrepresent our past achievements.

- Get bypassed for promotions or prized job assignments when others—our bosses or other decision makers—are unclear about or unaware of our accomplishments.

- Are unable to clearly establish our credentials in presentations or when selling.

- Are unaware of how to acquire invaluable "hidden" information needed to close sales when networking effectively. Yes – closing sales start with setting the context for *who* we are and *how* we have best served our previous customers/clients.

It's time to stand up and be valued!

The truth is, sharing your "brags," accomplishments," "achievements," "successes," and "wins" in a business-savvy manner makes the sales/marketing process, idea sharing, nomination writing for awards, and RFPs/RFQs/grant writing much more manageable and rewarding.

Your awareness and ability to communicate your achievements succinctly will improve your ability to write and speak more directly and confidently about what you do and what you can provide. This attracts the positive attention you need.

You're more likely to win the invitation to make a speech, conduct a sales presentation, or share your ideas. And you are more apt to have others want to hear about your products/services.

You could even receive the deserved award or recognition.

Since you can differentiate your business and product/service offerings with clarity, people are more likely to become "raving fans" and "tell others about you."

By valuing yourself and your successes, regardless of the size of them, you influence and inspire others, and build credibility. You feel great ... and so do others who listen to you. Don't believe me ... read *The Wall Street Journal* article noted on page 11. Then, complete the five easy steps outlined in this book.

It's time to *Get Your Brag On!* and start honoring your inner power!

Jeannette

INTRODUCTION

You have less than 4.3 minutes to create credibility at the beginning of *any* presentation.

You have less than 15 seconds to attract interest when networking.

It's up to you to create a remarkable, positive, and lasting impression.

Your success requires you to talk with others in a business-savvy manner.

All of us are taught at a very early age that bragging is wrong, especially the older generations of business professionals. It has been considered rude and showed poor manners if we shared our successes, wins, and accomplishments! If we do promote ourselves, the fear is we will be thought of as braggarts. Or worse, we fear being laughed at or ridiculed for our hubris (aka self-promotion).

Younger generations have the added peer pressure that no one can stand out from the crowd/group/team. Admitting you did something unique isn't something the team or group will applaud. It's become the "I" versus "we" controversy many people today are grappling with, regardless of whether others on the team did the work. The problem? Failure to say "I" hurts your credibility as a leader or boss, and using "we" doesn't tell others what you've accomplished and can be misleading.

Regardless of the "generation," we learned growing up that we must downplay our wins … often to our detriment. Especially, when others learn about our successes!

What happens when we fail to share our achievements with others?

How many times have you:

- Lost a sale, contract, or award, and the other company or person was less qualified?

- Failed to share successes you and your company have experienced?

- Been reminded not to be a braggart? Or, you need to "humble brag!" (Humble bragging is apologizing or diminishing a success before or after sharing it.)[2]

- Done a presentation and have the audience not "get" your unique ability to make a positive difference?

- Blamed the loss of business on your competition, your age or gender, or the economy?

- Left a sales presentation feeling defeated and depleted— your energy sapped?

- Resented being told you must promote yourself, believing people should know what you've done by your job title?

- Feeling it's nonsense to know your numbers and share them appropriately? (Hint: Every business owner must know their numbers!)

---

[2] Robson, David, "In praise of bragging", *The Wall Street Journal,* https://www.wsj.com/lifestyle/relationships/in-praise-of-bragging-f726b125, June 20, 2024.

Try on this idea: you fail to "win" because you're not getting your brag on. Or, you've relied on a slogan or long-winded talk about your company. (Hint: Your audience stopped listening quite a while ago and are busy looking at their phones or yawning.)

Many business professionals have been told not to share their successes for fear of offending someone. The problem? If a prospective client is unaware of your achievements and what you've accomplished, they will not ask you to "Tell me more." Hence, no sale or contract.

Challenges to recognize:

The first challenge: "Know, like, and trust" have become the foundation for building relationships in business and can be misleading. Too often, we fail to establish a business connection, and instead, we default to focusing on making friends. We also rely on social media connections to stay in touch personally and professionally. But if you're focused on making friends and not on developing new clients and business associates for lead generation, you're leaving a lot of money on the table.

The second challenge: People like to "brag" about the number of people they are connected to. But it doesn't tell the story about what they've accomplished and how they've helped others in their business endeavors. The number of connections is a detractor— there are highly successful people with a small number of "social media" contacts they do business with.

The third challenge: Our social media bios and resumes lack the information to differentiate us from others doing similar work (e.g., no two coaches, accountants, IT consultants, or other professionals in the same field do business the same way or have the same accomplishments). Often, we hide behind a company name or slogan instead of standing up and speaking up about who we are and what we've accomplished. We are unaware of our own brags.

When you are focused on making friends and not developing business relationships, you lose money and potential clients out of fear of not being liked or accepted!

What Gets in Your Way of Bragging?

The following are ways to lose out on current and future opportunities and access to business connections:

- Inability to distinguish or differentiate yourself with brevity and clarity about your achievements.

- Being too creative. People are unable to identify with or understand what you're saying.

- Using "safe words," or common and overused words, that are fluffy and meaningless (e.g., business professional, integrity, trustworthy, transformative).

- Failure to share your brags when setting up and conducting networking meetings out of fear that others won't like you or the other person will be offended. (It shows a lack of confidence or self-esteem.)

- Feel that winging a presentation or a networking meeting is authentic. (It's not! It simply shows you didn't care enough to do the work.)

- Failure to put down the electronics and other distractions while others talk. Multi-tasking is a myth. Those electronics have become status symbols that tell others "I'm too busy or important." (Definite conversation stoppers.)

- Fear of being in the spotlight. This reluctance stays with you although you have been overlooked for promotions, sales contracts, key job assignments, or industry recognition that you are qualified for.

- Not knowing your numbers—yes, many business professionals fail to track their financial and other results (aka metrics).

What Are You Waiting For?

- Wanting an epiphany or to feel comfortable, or less stressed, or less busy.

- Hoping to project confidence in the moment—but your lack of natural or forced confidence comes out in other ways (80 percent of communication is non-verbal). It can get in the way of people hearing what you're saying and how you can help them.

- Wanting to downplay or "dummy down" or "shrink" yourself and attempt "humble bragging" which includes apologizing before or after sharing a brag. (The habit of boasting with a complaint or false humility—it actually makes you less likable because you seem insincere.[3]) These beliefs get in the way of sharing your successes in a business-savvy manner. You will miss out on opportunities.

---

[3] Ovül Sezer at Cornell University's SC Johnson College of Business, quoted in Robson, David, "In praise of bragging", *The Wall Street Journal,* https://www.wsj.com/lifestyle/relationships/in-praise-of-bragging-f726b125, June 20, 2024.

> *"It ain't bragging if you've done it."*
> *– Walt Whitman*

It's Time to Get Real!

When you brag so others readily understand and value your results, your inner confidence and competence naturally speak volumes. People no longer dismiss your experiences and credentials and willingly listen to how you can make a positive difference in their business environment. (Note: If they don't see your value, move on. It's a waste of your time and energy to attempt to convince them.)

> *"When I met with the speaker from my last networking meeting, I was surprised by the depth and successes she'd achieved—I'm definitely looking forward to our next meeting to see how she can help me increase my business success."*
> *– BK, Business Consultant*
> *"P.S.: I bought her book too!"*

The critical ingredient to bragging effectively is authenticity and transparency (aka clarity). When you talk with network contacts (e.g., people you meet and connect with at a formal meeting, conference meet-and-greet, trade or meet-up event, etc.) or submit contract bids, you need to sound like the winner you are!

Three significant distinctions of meetings:

Introductory meetings are to let others know you exist. These meetings are NOT designed for selling! In 30 seconds to 2 minutes (typical networking or conference-style meetings), it's an opportunity to introduce yourself. 99.99 percent of people do NOT buy at that time. Unfortunately, I've listened to too many business professionals talk ad nauseum about themselves, their company, and their products for 2 to 5 minutes. They say nothing that differentiates them from everyone else, and everyone stops listening in the first 15 seconds. They have just lost an important opportunity that could have been avoided with the preparation of their "Brags!"

Networking meetings are marketing. Too often these meetings are done to check the box for yourself or to show your boss that you've been busy. The truth? You didn't conduct a networking meeting. Networking meetings are done virtually or face-to-face. They are not for selling! The purpose of such a meeting is getting to know the other person, the company, and the product/service. The focus is conducting research, educating yourself about different possibilities, and confidently sharing information to find out the 90 percent of "hidden" information not found on the company website. (SEE Chapter 10, Networking Works)

These meetings provide you with a deeper understanding of an industry, profession, or company while obtaining critical additional information that is often unwritten or is quickly spoken about. This is where "Know, Like, and Trust" **start** to get created. Your ability to follow through and follow up is essential to continue the process. (Note: When you fail to follow-up and follow-through via calls, emails, or texts or give up when there is no response (which is a frequent complaint by both sellers and buyers) you lose an opportunity to make a difference.)

Sales calls are for selling. You cannot effectively network and make a sales call at the same time … this is one of the biggest mistakes people make when meeting people for the first time. (Or frequently in networking meetings.) Remember, the value of the "unwritten" or "unspoken" information often helps you close the sale, win the contract or award, or make a positive impression. (SEE Chapter 10, Networking Works) (Note: Many fail to "brag" in their introductions and to effectively share brags during their presentations. "Let me think it over" is code for "No!")

Get Your Brag On! is designed to guide:

- Business Owners
- Entrepreneurs, Start-Ups, 1099 Contributors
- Gig workers wanting/needing to increase their "ratings"
- Consultants, Coaches, and Vendors
- Sales/Marketing/Customer Service Reps
- Executives and Board Members
- Trainers & Speakers
- Authors
- Those seeking recognition (government contracts, industry, trade awards, etc.)
- Those seeking investors and non-financial supporters
- And everyone else who wants to succeed at selling themselves

(Note: *Get Your Brag On!* is not intended to replace a qualified sales system, but it will enhance the process for achieving better results while building the required credibility and confidence during sales prospecting, presentations, and closing the deal.)

I attended a networking meeting and met a woman who shared with me two statements, the one she used to share at networking meetings and her new revised "brag" statement from attending one of my workshops.

Original statement: My company provides residential roofing.

Brag statement: I am a sales rep for a 34-year-old roofing company that has replaced over 35,000 roofs!

I was so impressed by the "brag" difference that when I met a realtor a few minutes later, I brought her over to meet the roofing company sales rep. The realtor was so impressed by the woman's "brag" statement that the realtor quickly provided two hot referrals!

The realtor later shared with me, "I've had those referrals for a couple of days and didn't know who to give them to."

I've seen this happen countless times. People are so impressed by effective bragging that they immediately offer referrals or want to schedule time to talk further.

It's time to get over your shyness, reluctance, and fear. It's time to learn how to make a positive and lasting impression.

In the following chapters, you will learn how to brag and:

- Share your accomplishments in a business-savvy manner
- Share your numbers and other metrics in a positive manner
- Establish immediate credibility and interest
- Sell yourself first with brevity and clarity in sales or networking meetings

- Provide clarity and differentiation in contract bids, award nominations, and sales proposals

- Develop a better understanding of a company's or industry's issues as a result of networking meetings *before* a sales call

- Be heard and be seen in a business-savvy way that compels others to take positive notice

Are you ready to *Get Your Brag On!?* Let's move forward!

1

Act Like a Cat

"If you can't sell yourself, you can't sell your ideas, products, or services ... or be taken seriously."
—Jeannette Seibly

The key purpose of *Get Your Brag On!* is to help you:

- Establish credibility immediately and in a professional manner
- Garner hidden information faster in networking meetings
- Set up and manage introductions for effective prospecting, presentations, and client meetings
- Impress judges with your value and accomplishments when reading your nomination for a business award or other recognition
- Differentiate yourself in sales proposals, contract bids, websites, brochures, social media, and marketing materials
- Ask for what you're worth
- Seek help, investors, and non-financial assistance
- And most of all, be seen as clear, confident, and competent

Why are these important? Because you are an amazing person with impressive accomplishments! (You should reread that statement several times and let it sink in.)

"We all need to share our greatness and be heard!"
– Sheryl Hickerson, CEO & Founder of Females & Finance

You are the cat. The purpose of this picture is to remind you how you look when you attempt to look like everyone else, sound like everyone else, or plagiarize others' accomplishments.

Too often, we pretend we are raccoons when, in fact, we're cats. Everyone knows we're cats. The raccoons realize we're not like them. The raccoons expect us to act like a cat when interacting with them. Obviously, as a cat, you can never be a raccoon.

Attempting to be something you are not is unimpressive, even when you act respectfully and tactfully. When you hide your true abilities and try to be like everyone else, it camouflages your accomplishments and uniqueness. Brags encourage others to want to learn more about you, and your product, service, ideas, or books. The biggest mistake you can make is mimicking others.

As often as I've shown this picture in my presentations, people miss seeing the difference between a cat and two raccoons! Many times, we don't necessarily hear the difference, either.

The point? People are less likely to talk with you and become interested in you (your ideas, products, services, and books) when they cannot distinguish any difference between you and the many others competing for their attention.

Too often, you will keep talking because you have misinterpreted the other person's glazed-over look—if you notice it at all—and mistake the look for interest in what you have to say. The other person becomes uncomfortable and will avoid you.

If you try to act and sound like everyone else, they will shut out everything you say and think, "I've heard it all before." Or, it reminds them of a bad experience with someone who sounded just like you.

Whenever you hear yourself starting to sound like everyone else, stop! Think of the cat and the raccoons. The picture is a friendly reminder that, too often, we like to hide out. It feels safer. However, hiding out won't pay the bills or earn you money or any well-deserved recognition. Nor will it win you a contract, award, or promotion. (If you're looking for a job, get your copy of *The Secret to Winning the Job: Start Bragging!*)

How do you show you're a winner?

How do you wow others subtly but clearly while sharing your accomplishments?

Keep reading. Complete the written exercises in this *Get Your Brag On! Business Edition*.

To be clear, you must do the work. Just reading the book won't get you out there bragging in a positive and powerful manner.

Here's the winning formula:

- First, Take the time to do the exercises.
- Second, Own your achievements.
- Third, Share your accomplishments with others.

A manager and her team were seated at a company function when her boss was called to the front of the room. The president of this multimillion-dollar marketing company acknowledged the boss for the work the manager and her team had accomplished. Imagine their surprise when the boss didn't mention them.

Later, one-on-one and in private, the manager asked her boss, "Why didn't you acknowledge me and the team?"

His only response was, "Someday, you will learn how to brag!"

While this is a boss with poor people management skills, the lesson is to Get Your Brag On! *and avoid these type of situations—which happen too often.*

2

The Key Ingredient

**"To brag effectively, be your own greatest advocate
in a confident, positive, and effective manner."**
—Jeannette Seibly

First, let me tell you a quick story (it's true with a name change)
that occurred when I wrote and published the first Brag! book
(*It's Time to Brag!*).

> *Mary, a professional speaker and trainer, called me because
> she was frustrated with not getting the speaking engagements
> she wanted—it was impacting her financial well-being. I shared,
> "I just released my "Brag!" book. Let me talk you through it."*
>
> *We went through the 5 easy steps.*
>
> *When we were done, she exclaimed, "That's stupid; it'll
> never work!"*
>
> *I replied, "Well, if you get hungry enough, you may wish to
> 'try' it."*
>
> *Now, imagine my surprise a couple of months later when I
> attended an event where she was the keynote speaker. She was
> oozing with credibility when the person introducing her handed
> her the mic to do her presentation.*

After Mary's presentation, people stood around her, wanting to know more about working with her.

When I was leaving, she caught my eye and mouthed, "Thank You!"

Below and on the next page, you will find two similar bios describing me, Jeannette Seibly, the author of this book. Read each one. Select the one you like best. Then, ask yourself if you can identify the key difference between them.

INTRODUCTION #1: About the Author

Jeannette Seibly is an internationally recognized talent advisor and executive coach who has worked with entrepreneurs, executives, and business owners. She has helped many people work smarter, enjoy financial freedom, and realize their dreams NOW.

She has an uncanny ability to help her clients identify roadblocks and focus on their goals to produce unprecedented results quickly. Each client has unique challenges, and Jeannette's gift is helping each one create success in their unique way.

She has guided the creation of millionaires and helped companies achieve million-dollar results.

Jeannette has a B.S. in personnel administration and an M.A. in communications from Michigan State University.

She has received many business and speaking awards.

INTRODUCTION #2: About the Author

Jeannette Seibly has been an internationally recognized talent advisor and leadership results coach for more than 32 years. She has helped thousands of entrepreneurs, executives, and business owners work smarter, enjoy financial freedom, and realize their dreams NOW.

Jeannette has an uncanny ability to help her clients identify roadblocks and focus quickly to produce unprecedented results. Each client has unique challenges and Jeannette's gift is helping each one create success in his or her own unique way. Along the way, she has guided the creation of three millionaires, helped more than 25 companies produce million-dollar results, and guided hundreds of business professionals to achieve six-figure incomes.

Jeannette has conducted more than 25 "Get Your Brag On!" workshops – one was recognized with the "People's Choice Award for Best Speaker," with standing room only on a Friday at 3:00 pm! (Society of Women Engineers—Regional Conference)

As an author, Jeannette has written eleven books; three have been recognized as international Amazon Best Sellers: *Hire Amazing Employees; The Secret to Selling Yourself Anytime, Anywhere: Start Bragging!;* and *The Old Wooden Rocker* (a novel).

She has published more than 700 articles on current management, entrepreneurial, and leadership challenges, in ten different business publications including the *Denver Business Journal* and General Motors *Consultant* and *Leadership* publications for dealerships.

Jeannette has a B.S. in personnel administration and an M.A. in communications from Michigan State University.

She has received four business awards from national groups for speaking, coaching, business growth, and sales growth.

Which one did you like best? Which sounded more professional? Which created credibility faster than the other one? Which one pulled you into the conversation sooner?

Most people will say #2.

What is the critical difference? Many people have a difficult time distinguishing the difference. They'll say, "Sounds more specific." "It's more interesting." "It's more descriptive." Everything is similar except for one key ingredient!

What is it?

The second bio contained numbers, metrics, and results.

It bragged!

3

Share Your Accomplishments

"If you sound like everyone else, nobody will listen."
—Jeannette Seibly

When you present your results in a businesslike manner, it lets people know that you're a winner. People like to work with winners.

So, why are people not listening to or interested in you?

They don't readily understand how you can help them. People today have short attention spans. They stop listening if you get too creative (e.g., using jargon, fancy words, or made-up descriptions), use big or meaningless words, or are self-deprecating. If you're boring, they stop listening. If you talk on and on, they look at their phones, hoping you'll stop talking.

They don't know how or lack the interest to ask the right questions to clarify. Or, when they do, you start over again with the same old rhetoric, repeating yourself and hoping they'll get the value the second (or third) time around.

The challenge is sharing the difference you provide so that people want to listen.

It's sharing your accomplishments in a business-savvy manner.

Relying on rhetoric obtained from websites (you will lose sales opportunities by telling someone to go to your website to learn about you and your products/services instead of directly answering their questions), self-help books, or sales and marketing workshops will not differentiate you from others with the same or a similar background, experience, and education. Showcasing your credentials in a business-savvy manner is vital to ensure people are interested in talking with you further.

Remember, salespeople, consultants, business owners, executives, and entrepreneurs often believe their company is unique. If you get too creative as a way of distinguishing yourself, nobody understands you. If they don't readily understand you or you are unable to talk in basic business terms, they may question your business acumen and infer a lack of knowledge or integrity on your part.

The exercises in the upcoming chapters will address the following questions:

- What are your accomplishments?

- What differentiates or sets you apart from others?

- What do your past or current clients respect you for?

- What are the positive and profound differences you have made for your bosses, coworkers, clients, and in personal and professional activities?

- What is the secret to bragging and self-promotion for you?

Remember, trying to be a raccoon when you're a cat will not help you succeed.

The following is a paraphrased testimonial from a former client who is a serial entrepreneur.

HJ started two businesses and failed because he could not differentiate his successes effectively. Investors were not interested! After doing the exercises in this book, HJ sold his third and fourth businesses quickly and for more money than anticipated. He's now selling business number five!

His feedback: "I have always been impressed by people who are good at telling others what they accomplished in their career ... these people seemed amazing to me.
When I wrote down and explained what I was good at ... looked at my own accomplishments ... I started to look pretty amazing myself."
– HJ, a serial entrepreneur

As a business owner, entrepreneur, consultant, sales or marketing rep, author, or someone looking to win industry recognition, you can accomplish what you want when you learn to brag.

You're often unconscious of what you do, how well you do it, and the difference it makes for employers, clients, communities, readers, or others. You simply focus on getting the task done. You repeat the rhetoric heard at a recent event. You tell people what you did for your past clients—not as accomplishments, but as tasks. Or, you share numbers without results—which fails to convey their importance. This does not tell the story of your true accomplishments.

It's like reading the back book cover describing a book and believing you've read the story before. But when you actually read the story, you find differences galore.

In the past, when I introduced myself, if asked what I did, I would say, "I am a coach." Too often, that would be the end of any conversation since there are thousands of coaches today. It didn't convey anything new. There was nothing to differentiate me from the other thousand coaches. I failed to brag!

However, now I say, "I'm a Leadership Results Coach with more than 32 years of experience, and along the way, I have guided the creation of three millionaires."

I have their attention. It provides a differentiation. The statement invites them to continue the conversation. If they are interested in learning more, they will ask questions to start a dialogue. If not, I move on and talk with someone who is interested.

Remember, talking with someone not interested in what you do is not time well spent. Think, are you busy making new friends or increasing your financial, business, or intended results? In business, you establish relationships instead of striving to make new friends.

Some of you may think I'm talking about refining your elevator pitch. I'm not. It's more than that. It requires *authentically* being aware of and *owning* your achievements. It's getting into the pages of this book and learning how to share your story in a quick and effective manner. Although you still need a brag one-liner, an objective is required to get their attention. (SEE Chapter 6, Step Four: I Am …)

If you are not already bragging (which is probably why you are reading this book) don't attempt to short-cut the process or force the result without doing the work contained in *Get Your Brag On!* You risk sounding stilted, and overlooking some of your distinguishing accomplishments. Without understanding how amazing you are, you also risk not having your natural inner confidence shine through.

When you've completed the exercises in *Get Your Brag On!*, you'll have a supporting paragraph ready to share with others.

- It provides credibility and talks about your successes.

- It elicits interest and makes others want to learn more.

- It increases the possibility others will want to work with you.

- It gets you selected!

- It gets you referred to great opportunities!

- It naturally builds your confidence and inspires others. And your inner confidence naturally shines, expands, and attracts others to you!

- It allows you to see what you've accomplished.

It is the first step in learning how to brag in a businesslike manner. You win and feel like a winner! (Not a fraud or imposter!) This entire process will create a huge breakthrough for you.

Are you ready to start bragging?

At a book event, one author was going to read a script on her phone to pitch to a group of potential readers. After five minutes of reworking her introduction and speaking from her heart, she was bragging! She wowed them and sold all of the books she'd brought to the event. (An accomplishment she continues to achieve at other events.) Even the hostess, a publishing expert, was amazed and impressed by her pitch.

Remember, luck is in your preparation.
Are you prepared?
Let's get started!

4

Ready? Let's Start!

"Are you ready? Remember, getting started is the hardest part of the process!"
—Jeannette Seibly

Here are the five steps:

- Knowledge, Talents, Achievements (KTAs)
  (Steps One through Three) Chapter 5

- I am … (Step Four) Chapter 6

- My background includes … (Step Five) Chapter 7

- The key is to keep writing, it's one of the secrets to creating memorable brags.

- Don't stop after writing down a couple of things.

- Keep writing!

- When you think you're done, keep writing!

- When you can't think of the answers, keep writing.

- Trust the process—the breakthroughs will come through your writing.

The written exercises are designed to put structure in uncovering your wins, successes, and achievements. It's to move your thinking toward discovering what you have accomplished. You will be amazed by (and in awe of) the results.

The key is to keep it simple, and not to make it more complicated than it is. Keep writing, even when you think you're finished or cannot think of anything to write. I promise there is more there to be written down.

Don't be fooled by the simplicity of the exercises. Many people have been and, consequently, didn't do the work to create their brags or allowed their reluctance to get in the way. When you do the writing, there is an authenticity or transparency that you cannot fake.

While I've had people set aside the exercises, and eventually start again, I've also had people cry out of frustration. Why? Many people experience reluctance in writing anything down. But eventually, they had a breakthrough. They were on their way to bragging and promoting themselves as successful winners.

It's all in the writing. It's getting your brain to realize your accomplishments by making you conscious of them. It forces you to get present to your results. And it allows you to recognize the impacts you've had, which many of us are unaware of.

Regardless of your age or life experiences, you've accomplished many things. Write them all down. (Note: Many of you, particularly Millennials and GenZ, may want to type. Consider, studies have shown that writing down your responses engages your brain differently, helping you connect with what you are putting down on paper and have already accomplished in your career and life.) If you're unable to write, use whatever method works best for you.

This five-step process allows you to become conscious of them. It helps you to recognize yourself as a successful business professional.

Do the written work. Stay out of your mental monologues. No one else will see this work unless, of course, you show them.

Remember, shortcuts rarely have any lasting effects.

5

Steps One, Two, and Three: KTAs
(Knowledge, Talents, Achievements)

"Recognizing your value can actually be a lot of fun."
—Jeannette Seibly

Step One:
Knowledge: What do you know?

The chart on the following pages contains ideas to get you started. They are not inclusive. Use your own ideas or business groupings that have meaning for you. The breakthrough will only be as good as the writing you do. If you are unable to write, have someone else scribe for you. Or use transcription software that writes down what you are saying.

There are KTA worksheets in the back of this book. Or, you can download them on my website: https://SeibCo.com/KTA/

Knowledge*	Talents	Achievements
Sales		
Marketing		
Technology		
Project Management		
Software		
Engineering		
Consulting		
Operations		
International		
Finance		
Compliance		
Cybersecurity		
Human Resources		
Author		
Parenting		
Grandparenting		
Accounting		
Financial Reporting		
Perennial Gardening		
Cake Decorating		
Jewelry		
Non-Profit		
Attorney		
Student		

*Knowledge should ONLY be one or two words.

Again, the above are simply examples to get you started. See how many you can create!

Step Two:

Talent: Use a verb to describe each Knowledge. Feel free to include more than one!

Write down at least one Talent to describe each Knowledge (yes, you can have more than one). Talents are described using a verb and in only one to four words. (Note: The following are select examples of Knowledge and Talents.)

Knowledge*	Talents	Achievements
Sales	Lead Generation Prospecting Closing Handling Virtual Sales Respond to Customer Complaints	
Marketing	Branding Talk with Prospects Create Logos	
Technology	Sales Coding Website Development Create Apps	
Project Management	Coordinate Events Conduct Quarterly Client Reviews	
Software	Developing AI Programs Testing	

*Knowledge should ONLY be one or two words.

Knowledge*	Talents	Achievements
Engineering	Surveying Conduct Cost Analysis	
Human Resources	Hire Coach Manage Communicate Benefit Changes	
Author	Write Publish Market Contribute Articles	
Accounting	Set Up Excel Spreadsheets Create P&Ls	
Financial Planning	Set up Retirement Accounts	
Parenting	Coach Little League Fundraising	
Grandparenting	Babysit Adopt Cats Foster Dogs	
Perennial Gardening	Create Flower Beds	
Cake Decorating	Create Kids Cakes Organize Wedding Receptions	

*Knowledge should ONLY be one or two words.

Knowledge*	Talents	Achievements
Jewelry	Work with Metal Beading	
Non-Profit	Create 501(c)3 Fundraising Host Monthly Board Meetings	

Attorney	Resolve Employment
	   Claims
	Create Business
	   Contracts
	Resolve Probate
	   Matters	

Student	Tutor Talk with Others Participate in Team Sports	

*Knowledge should ONLY be one or two words.

Again, the above are simply examples to get you started. See how many you can create!

Step Three:
Achievements: Use two numbers to show your results.

Achievements are the secret to getting people to hear you and wanting to learn more about your successes.

The key is using two numbers to show the results you've achieved that made a positive difference and produced results.

Simply talking about a task isn't inspiring to others. Too often, business websites or people's resumes will say, "Troubleshoot software issues. Handled day-to-day challenges. Sold cars. Top salesperson. Handled administrative work for the company president." These don't tell us anything unique. There is no differentiation. They're examples of *being a cat while attempting to look like a raccoon!* They fail to brag and share your successes.

Achievements and results are why people hire you, want to do business with you, and why companies consider you a top performer.

Don't worry if your mind freezes when thinking about numbers, metrics, or key performance indicators (KPIs). Many might say, "I don't need to know my numbers." But as business professionals, we do need to know our numbers. Why? Because numbers sell! They subtly communicate our industry experience, professional wins, and tangible results. So, embrace the power of numbers in your professional journey.

Numeric results and other metrics require getting into the details of what you have accomplished.

Becoming aware of what you've accomplished allows you to see your positive impact and honor the results you've produced, either on your own or with a team.

Doing this level of work makes you more proficient when communicating your accomplishments, even though you will not be communicating all the details.

When you communicate unconsciously, you tend to be glib and gloss over important points. Or speak in a manner others don't understand. Or, share mind-numbing details. Or mumble, failing to stand up and speak up about your successes.

After completing these exercises, you will naturally communicate more consciously, sharing work and life experiences in a way others can relate to. You'll be inspiring and cause others to want to have meaningful conversations with you. This is how relationships and trust are created. It helps you get the sales contract, keep current clients, win contract bids or nominations, get promoted, successfully pitch a new idea or product, or secure great work assignments. For authors, it helps sell books.

For each Talent, write an Achievement using two numbers. The following are ideas to get you started. They are not inclusive. The breakthrough will only be as good as the writing you do. Don't let fear about your math ability get in the way.

If you are feeling stuck or feeling anxious, take a moment to breathe and become present with what you have written thus far. Remember, your brain is not trained to be mindful of your accomplishments, wins, successes, achievements, and awards. This is why it can be challenging to brag and self-promote you.

The following chart (on the next page) shows select "Achievements" (aka brags) and is an example. Write down many Achievements as you can for yourself and use two numbers to describe the results.

KTAs		
Knowledge	**Talents**	***Achievements** ***Use 2 numbers! These can be** **whole numbers, fractions,** **percentages, etc.**
Sales	Handling Virtual Sales	#1 company sales award for Q3 selling 10 luxury cars.
Software	Testing	Worked with a $10 Million-dollar client when a $150,000 software package failed to produce the results promised, and resolved the issues within three hours.
Engineering	Surveying	Conducted 10 surveys for the state highway department and saved $2M on one project.
Human Resources	Hire	Worked with a $20M company to reduce their 42% turnover down to 26% in 6 months, saving more than $250,000.
Parenting	Fundraising	Top seller of 100 candy bars and earned $500 for the 4-H chapter's trip to Washington, D.C.

KTAs		
Knowledge	**Talents**	***Achievements** ***Use 2 numbers! These can be** **whole numbers, fractions,** **percentages, etc.**
Non-Profit	Create 501(c)3	With no money, created the first Job Summit Association in 3 months and held four profitable events.
Attorney	Resolve Probate Matters	Worked with 3 siblings to resolve a $1M estate, and the siblings still get together each year on Thanksgiving.
Student	Tutor	Coached 4 friends through Calculus, 2 of them achieved an A.
	Talk with Others	Supported 2 friends during a 24-hour mental health breakdown.
	Participate in Team Sports	Played QB for 2 years.

Keep writing! **Many of you will not readily know your numbers.** That's not a problem. Write down your thoughts. After you are done writing, conduct research with former coworkers or bosses, clients (don't forget past ones—it's a great way to reconnect), business associates, trade association contacts, and service professionals (CPAs, attorneys, consultants, etc.).

Although most people will not investigate your numbers, you want to be as truthful as possible. If you are caught in a lie, it could easily hurt your ability to attract new opportunities or win recognition from your employer or be recognized by an outside organization.

As one participant said after struggling with numbers, "We all have numbers to describe our successes. It's simply becoming present to the difference we made and the results we accomplished."

The key to completing Steps One through Three? Stay out of mental monologues or excuses telling you this is too hard, you don't like working with numbers, or you don't believe you should have to do the work. Writing this information down will show you what you've accomplished thus far in your life. *This information is priceless!*

Get Your Brag On! *is a critical tool to develop not only the ABILITY to Brag, but also to unlock the WILLINGNESS to Brag.*
— Ellen Burnes, Ph.D.
Independent Board Director and Finance Professor

Remember, you've got years of false conditioning telling you it's not OK to brag or it's poor business manners to share your successes and achievements. Now is the time to blast through those limiting walls that have hindered your career, business recognition, and professional and industry credibility.

When I worked with a group of job seekers age 50+, this exercise created the "deer-in-headlights" look.

They were not experienced at selling themselves.

They believed hiring managers should know by reading their resume what they had achieved ... they shouldn't need to promote themselves or brag.

The problem is, people are not mind readers ... you need to tell them.

Shameless self-promotion is key to winning the job.

The fact that you are aware of your numbers (a.k.a. results) and can communicate them appropriately will provide you with the advantage. Doing so will set you apart from the pack and help you differentiate yourself from others unable to share their results. *It's being the cat with a satisfied grin that s/he is a cat instead of pretending to be a raccoon. While you may run into others with similar backgrounds, it's rare to see or hear of anyone with exactly the same experiences and achievements. You're unique—showcase it.*

Let me offer you some tips on how to think about your numbers. Remember, numbers can be expressed in percentages, actual numbers, and approximations (i.e., realistic guesstimates). Not everything is quantifiable; for example, it is difficult to measure employees' happiness even though that may interest some people. However, you can quantify your results by looking at the outcomes or results that occurred when employees experienced job satisfaction and the company increased employee retention.

An estate attorney was struggling with her brags since most people are not "happy" about working through estate matters after a loved one's death. The brag? "I worked with more than 100 clients, and 50% of them still get together at the Thanksgiving table!" Keep in mind, on average, more than 95 percent of estate settlements are contentious.

Most prospective clients and business associates will be most interested in how many projects or consulting engagements you achieved on time and within budget.

- What was the budget? Timeframe?
- How long did it take to actually complete the project while working with and through others?
- What were the challenges with team members, and how did you overcome them?
- What other setbacks arose?
- How did you handle them?
- Did you have any turnover?

These things can be measured and tell the story of what was accomplished in a succinct and inspiring manner.

You may be resistant or challenged by this part of the exercise—many people are. Keep writing! I had one woman cry through the whole exercise, but she persisted. Within two weeks, she was re-employed after being unemployed for 18 months.

6

Step Four: I Am …

"Effectively communicate who you are and the value you provide."
—Jeannette Seibly

Don't work on this Step until you've completed several pages of the KTAs (Knowledge, Talents, and Achievements). (See the back of this book for worksheets.)

In 20 words or less, describe who you are. Keep it simple and smart.

Start with the phrase, "I am …"

- Make it easy for people to understand you. Talk straight and stay away from using jargon, slang, cutesy, or fancy words. When people don't readily understand you or aren't able to connect with you, they will move on instead of wanting to learn more. Also, avoid overusing words that many other people use (e.g., integrity, trustworthy, coach, team player, business professional, etc.). People will stop listening thinking they've heard it before.

- As a rule, ask yourself if a 12-year-old could easily understand your words.

- If you MUST explain to be understood, it's not simple enough. Simple and smart brag statements create interest in you.

- If you have to explain, many people assume you are being defensive or talking down to them—another reason people stop listening.

For example, I could say, "I am a coach who helps others get out of their way." But there are no numbers and it is not enough to generate interest in how I can help someone because it is generic and there are thousands of coaches with similar brags.

However, if I say, "I am a business advisor who has guided the creation of three millionaires," I've created interest with struggling business owners. Or, if I say, "I'm a management consultant who helped one company reduce turnover from 125 percent to 25 percent," I have the attention of the business owner who is experiencing expensive turnover issues.

Avoid clichés like "I help people feel great!" or "I help companies become successful." These statements are overused and don't tell the listener anything specific about your accomplishments and fail to build credibility.

Be clear what you do. For example, if you're a salesperson seeking a promotion, you might say, "I am a sales professional and surpass my quota by 25 percent each quarter."

If you are a consultant who conducts customer service training, you could say, "I am a customer service rep who achieves 100 percent customer satisfaction." (I helped a young man who had been waiting tables win a job offer to be a customer service rep with this one.)

Sharing your unique qualities generates interest in learning more. Focus on what you have successfully accomplished with your current and past clients (and previous employers), this specific information will be of interest to your prospective client.

(Critical note: Never share confidential information.)

Unless someone asks you a question, providing additional information after you've made your initial statement is like talking to the wall. They are not listening! Wait until a question is asked and answer it directly with the information on your background that you developed. (SEE Chapter 7, Step Five: My Background Includes …)

Plan to fine-tune this all-important "I am …" statement. You may need to test it out on several people. Work with a business coach or a marketing or PR friend to help you. (Note: Do not let them talk you out of using your numbers. Numbers sell you. Metrics differentiate you from the competition. Facts help you win.)

Some of you will be frustrated; this information doesn't necessarily come out the first time you write it down. Or the second time. Or the third. Remember that in most cases, your brain has been trained to hide out and play small. Or, if you are uncomfortable talking straight, you've trained your brain to spin the facts or be highly creative. Although this may help satisfy your ego, it won't help you attract positive attention. Being genuine builds relationships that begin by talking and sharing information that enables the other person to readily understand you.

Make sure you're using simple business words that are easily identifiable: "business advisor," "executive coach," "sales representative for a software engineering company," "virtual assistant for executives," "estate attorney," "business owner," or "CPA."

These often-used business titles help others to easily identify what you do. Again, stay away from cute or faddish jargon or acronyms. Using creative job titles can actually be off-putting since people don't readily know what you do and don't feel comfortable asking.

In addition to attracting new clients, straight talk can also produce promotions or new opportunities. This requires completing the brag exercises.

Many sales reps, unconsciously or due to a lack of hands-on experience, misrepresent their companies' products and services. Imagine how frustrated you would be if you started a conversation with something like "I'm looking for a financial consultant," and only after further conversation did you learn that the consultant (or their company) didn't have the required financial experience or technology, and was trying to sell you investments that you didn't have an interest in.

Learn your trade and understand the details of what you are selling and how the process works. As one successful person shared after creating two million-dollar businesses, "Know the details of your products and services—it can turn a maybe into a yes."

Talk straight when creating and using your "I am …" statement.

7

Step Five: My Background Includes …

"Stand up, speak up, and don't let others diminish your value."
—Jeannette Seibly

Step Five is where you bring it all together. Write one to two paragraphs about your background that describe and support your "I am …" statement. Customize them for the audience. USE the NUMBERS!!!

Keep it short and to the point. Write out several different versions. Then, practice them in front of the mirror. Don't be afraid to change it now or in the future as needed.

Stop editing yourself while you are talking! Otherwise, you will start with one short paragraph, but keep talking and repeating yourself. It loses everyone's attention.

Most people, including decision-makers, have short attention spans. If you're unable to grab their attention quickly, you will probably not receive the contracts or nominations you wanted, or an introduction to the right person within a targeted company.

Write a well-worded paragraph or two in the email you send after you've met with someone as a reminder about your specific success and to generate further interest.

Customize your background statement for your audience and use those numbers. It's amazing to me that we spend time clarifying results with numbers and then don't use them.

You may wish to review my two bios in Chapter 2. In the first one, I didn't use numbers, but in the second, I did—it bragged!

In a sales presentation, tailor your introductory "brag" paragraphs to your listener's needs. Keep it to less than a minute. I remember one time when a person talked for 15 minutes during a sales introduction when presented with: "Tell us about yourself and your company." We were all so bored with him that the outcome was determined before the sales presentation even started: NO!

In a request for proposal (RFP) or request for quotation (RFQ), be sure to address the requirements upfront. Again, use your numbers to demonstrate your achievements (and those of the company). Remember, many contract bids are awarded to companies that follow the outline they provide while also providing the wow! factor. They brag and are unafraid to share their successes in a way that makes the reader want to know more.

You may wish to hire a business coach, PR person, or sales/marketing person to help you write or edit. Do not allow them to replace the numbers. They may not have learned how to brag yet. But the reality is they may feel uncomfortable working with numbers.

Or, you could have a raving fan of your talents (for example, a coworker, client, or boss) write it up for you, and then you can edit it.

Resist the urge to dumb it down! This means stop diminishing your value so that others feel comfortable with you. This is a common issue with women who are successful and fear others will feel intimidated by them. I have spoken with several people who are afraid to use their PhD on their LinkedIn bios or share coveted awards. The problem? When the client, friend, or business associate finds out (and they will), they will feel uncomfortable with you or believe you've withheld important information, which creates suspicion about what else you've failed to share.

Remember, it's how you talk to people that makes the difference. Learn to gauge your audience and talk about what's of interest to them, using words they can readily understand (e.g., generous versus magnanimous).

Don't forget to post these introductions on your social media pages. I've had many people tell me about how impressive my introductions are. (I've even won the Best Introduction award with a leads group.) This builds immediate credibility when having voice-to-voice conversations with them. During the discussion, I shared additional achievements that meet their interests.

The point? Take the time to write and fine-tune. Remember, your statement must be modified depending on the company, industry, or profession of the person you are talking with. Take time to network with others to find out what essential qualities the business you're interested in requires that are not listed on their website, PR posts, and other product/service information.

For example, if you are a consultant making a presentation to a group of small business owners about practical tips for hiring the right salesperson, it is not the same as speaking to a group of sales managers wanting to learn about motivational techniques.

Tailor your introduction accordingly. Don't forget: It's critical to build credibility in order for people to listen to your message. It makes all the difference in how they will listen to you—openly or with skepticism. It creates a context and helps keep the conversation focused—also known as achieving your intended results!

Remember, each "I am ..." statement may require different "My background includes ..." statements.

Here's an example using "I am ..." and "My background includes ..."

I am a Leadership Results Coach with 32 years of experience. My background includes guiding the creation of 3 million-aires and countless 6-figure income business professionals, from $1 million to $30 million in business revenues. My focus when working with these bosses and leaders is using state-of-the-art assessments tools and focusing on hiring, coaching, and managing practices to ensure their teams achieve the intended results.

8

Practice, Practice, Practice

**"When you share your accomplishments
with credibility, you become an influencer!"**
—Jeannette Seibly

Like anything, bragging or mastery of bragging takes practice.
Don't beat yourself up if you stumble or take the easy road by
not using your numbers.

Simply review and practice in front of the mirror. Keep doing
your "mirror work" until the person looking back at you in the
mirror gets it. If this was easy to do, I wouldn't have spent time
writing a book about it.

> *I met a young professional wishing to be a realtor. She had
> the education and licenses. However, when she talked with
> people, she looked at her feet! She purchased the first edition of
> the brag book,* It's Time to Brag! *and completed the five steps.
> The next time I saw her, she made eye contact, shook my hand
> confidently, and clearly articulated her successes in helping
> others find their dream homes. She had learned how to brag,
> and her new confidence radiated! So did her sales—she became
> a nationally recognized producer.*

You may get frustrated. You may be resistant. You may wish to be the cat trying to look like the raccoons—because it feels more comfortable. However, eventually, you'll get hungry enough to want the breakthrough. To be seen as the success you know you are.

If it feels too challenging, take small steps. Write down only one KTA each day. Share it with only one person per day.

You may have insights about accomplishments while you are driving to an appointment or lying in bed at night. Write them down. This flood of additional information may help you in your next networking meeting or on your next sales call or conversation with a current or future client. It can even help you with your boss. (No, clients and bosses don't know all the results you've achieved for the company.)

The goal is to have people better understand who you are and identify with what you can provide for them. Understanding yourself builds credibility faster. It will set the tone for your success.

During any type of presentation, you should plan to use your KTAs to help answer your prospective client's questions. Or, you can include them in your nomination for an industry award. A little bit of repetition, such as using the same set of numbers or examples, can help if you need to restate a particular point. But don't overdo it.

When writing sales copy, since consumers only skim it, be sure your first paragraph summarizes your and/or the company's achievements along with the numbers. You want to entice people to read further. If you're creating a website or brochure as an entrepreneur or small business owner, use your numbers and showcase your personal achievements. I think you get the idea.

You can also use the brag method to build your department, team, or business unit's sense of team loyalty. What have you achieved as a group? What are your unique qualities or areas of expertise? Voicing those accomplishments is also a great reminder of all the successful results you and the team have had. Don't forget to share them with a client who has shown signs of straying to your competition (SEE Chapter 12, Attracting New Clients).

This process works! When you share your brag statements, be responsible for your tone of voice, ego, and attitude. Coming across as a braggart, regardless of whether you're a professional woman or a man, will not help you. Coming across apologetically or mumbling will not work either. Jumping around and waving your arms exclaiming you're great and wonderful will only have others feel sorry for you.

Just share your successes in a straightforward and confident manner. Ensure your attitude is positive and helpful. Keep it simple. Humility and facts go a long way towards selling yourself.

Stay away from sharing any details regarding how you achieved the numbers until you get to that point in your presentation or are asked the question during a networking meeting. Then, stay away from the mind-numbing details of each minute step—remember, you want them to hire you to do the work, not to train them how to do it themselves.

The goal is for business associates and prospective customers to appreciate your expertise and to hear how you (and/or your company) helped others fix an issue or pursue an opportunity. They need to understand how you can do the same for them, their clients, or other companies they know based on their needs. This level of conversation is normally required before being offered an introduction to people or companies needing your products or services.

People want to work with winners.
Winners know how to share their achievements
in a professional manner that works.
Bragging is an important skill to fine-tune.

Your ability to communicate your successes using numbers will forever alter the way you think and speak and the way people relate to you.

You will probably see results quickly.

Have fun sharing.

Enjoy bragging!

Remember, you've earned your bragging rights. Share them in a business savvy manner and watch your credibility naturally rise!

9

Conduct Your Preliminary Research

"Always be prepared!"
—Jeannette Seibly

Too often, in our haste and because of poor planning, we fail to stop and consider the purpose of our networking meetings. We attempt to "wing it" and either fail to take the time to prepare or think it won't matter. Always take the time to conduct preliminary research before, not during, your meetings.

Be open to the fact that those you talk to may have a different goal or view of what they need. Be prepared to refer them to more appropriate vendors when opportunities present themselves during networking meetings, with their permission.

The biggest mistake many make when networking is promising they can deliver a product or service for a particular purpose that does not match what the company needs.

Before the Meeting

Read the individual's LinkedIn page and do an online search of their name to see what is posted. Also search on the name of the company and its products and services. If this is a potential client, not an introductory meeting, contact one or two people in your network for information that is not published. Remember, 90 percent of the world's information is in other people's heads! Check out the company's and your contact's social media information (e.g., LinkedIn, Facebook, etc.). Subscribe to their feeds to see what you can learn about their products and services.

Prepare, prepare, prepare!

10

Networking Works

**"Do you want to increase your financial results?
Create real networking meetings that
produce real results!"**
—Jeannette Seibly

Now that you've done your KTAs, written your I Am statement, and prepared My Background Includes, you are ready to get your brag on. Getting results with your brags often requires the following four steps:

1. Conducting research
2. Scheduling and attending networking meetings
3. Having meaningful conversations
4. Closing the sale

What is networking? Many think of networking as simply meeting others and listening to them pitch their products and services. They couldn't be further from the truth.

Savvy networkers know it's more than that.

Networking is talking with others to:

- Investigate new possibilities

- Become aware of new types of opportunities

- Explore new opportunities such as:
  - new technologies
  - new companies
  - new products
  - new occupations
  - new human relations/diversity concerns
  - environmental changes
  - ethical considerations
  - business awareness

The challenge is that 90 percent of the world's information is in people's heads! Unlocking what you need to know requires having conversations beyond text or social media blurbs. Put down the phone and electronic messaging and meet with others face to face, or if geography prohibits that, meet using a conferencing system.

Changes in business are occurring at the speed of light, and staying current and focused is important. Don't forget that new possibilities are being created daily. Find a niche for your skills and interests since you can't be everything to everyone. Then, learn everything you can, read trade journals, and subscribe to social media groups.

Showcase your expertise and stay focused. However, be careful about using slang or terminology in areas that are not your expertise. I've seen business professionals lose credibility quickly by misusing phrases, jargon, acronyms, or slang.

In order to network effectively you need to:

- Educate yourself about new opportunities

- Explore opportunities and conduct due diligence

- Connect with others for information regarding best practices and policies, critical issues, best technology to use, possible solutions, etc.

- Create new opportunities for yourself by staying current on upcoming challenges and possible solutions

- Evaluate options and be prepared to negotiate or pitch knowledgeably (SEE Chapter 14, Negotiate and Chapter 15, Pitching Your Products/Services/Books/Ideas)

- Make better decisions about future opportunities as they relate to your company and industry

- Make vying for a contract easier when you understand what they are really looking for, not what you are assuming they should be seeking

What are the added benefits of networking?

- Develops lifelong contacts so you can have great career success now and in the future

- Keeps you up to date on industry and professional changes

- Allows you to achieve your personal and professional goals faster

- Guides you to resolve issues more quickly and effectively

- Provides you with information on unpublished leads and career opportunities

- Connects you with others engaged in new ventures

Why do we make networking difficult? We are unclear about the difference between networking and selling. An important distinction to keep in mind: You cannot network and sell at the same time.

What's the difference between marketing and sales?

Marketing is:

- Researching issues and solutions
- Collecting information necessary to sell
- Finding new opportunities
- Educating yourself and others

Sales is:

- Presenting (i.e., sharing on-point solutions to clients' key issues and challenges)

- Conducting due diligence (i.e., knowing your potential customer's ability to pay, talking with the right decision-makers, uncovering hidden issues)

- Closing the deal (i.e., negotiating the terms of the deal and signing the contract)

Fine-tune your clarity:

- You cannot sell and market at the same time.

- You can't sell if you don't understand the company's needs (i.e., do your market research).

- Companies buy for their own reasons, not yours.

The purpose of networking is to tap into the unpublished information that often is a decisive factor because potential clients do not freely share all their concerns. They expect you to already know about the industry and its professional challenges and opportunities. It's why it's important to keep developing relationships. Remember, it's a two-way street—be available to help others too.

How to Do It

To keep your power and confidence, it's important that you come prepared for a networking meeting! Doing so increases your opportunity to trade information and learn about the person you are meeting with, his or her company, the profession, and the industry. Understanding and preparation on your part also prevents the person you're talking to from making a snap judgment about your product/service/idea.

(Important Note: Do not take or leave behind a brochure at a networking meeting or expect the potential client to check out your website to answer their questions. **Answer them!** Brochures, websites, and other materials are intended to support your conversations, presentations, and proposals not sell for you. They don't replace the need for conversation. Failure to understand this important point will limit future opportunities with the person you're talking to and with his or her company.)

DO TAKE your business cards and offer them to the people you meet in face-to-face meetings, or use electronic or digital business cards. Then, follow up within 24 hours by emailing a short note to say, "It was a pleasure to meet you." Stay away from announcing your meetings on social media venues—it can leave the other person feeling uncomfortable working or talking with you.

Keys to Conducting Effective Networking Meetings:

- You are establishing contacts that are valuable sources of information.

- You are seeking information regarding issues and potential solutions.

- You are building a network base for future business.

- You are building your lists of social media contacts. (Remember, the number of contacts will not help you— it's the quality of the connections.)

How Do You Get Started?

Networking can be daunting if you forget the basic tenets of how to share, how to listen, and common courtesies (e.g., saying please and thank you).

Make It Easy:

- Start conversations with:
  - former bosses
  - current and previous coworkers, vendors, and suppliers
  - past and current clients
  - trade association contacts
  - professional and personal acquaintances
  - social network contacts

Remember:

- Geography is not important.
- Check out social media sites and websites to supplement conversations with others.

- Face-to-face meetings or video conferencing is required to develop an ongoing connection.

How to Initiate a Meeting:

- Send an introductory email or message on LinkedIn or other social media platforms. Or, better yet, pick up the phone and call. You can also send a letter or email requesting a meeting. Sometimes, people will prefer texts or other messaging venues.

- If you use email or text, keep it short—a couple of paragraphs is optimal. In the Subject line, include "Referred by ..." or "Requesting a Meeting."

- If you're making a phone call, use a written script that you have practiced.

- If you're writing a letter, keep it short—no longer than one page. Be sure to proofread it! (Well-written letters can work to initially engage high-level people since they are bombarded with so many people wanting their time and attention.) Sending a letter or well-designed postcard via postal service can be a great way to attract someone's attention.

- When introducing yourself, do not attempt to sell! This is off-putting; often, the person will make a "yes" or "no" decision on whether or not to talk with you. Remember, while they may not need your products or services, they have contacts that may need you! But you won't get to them without a conversation.

- NEVER include a brochure or other type of attachment. Prospects will glance at it and say no and probably never open it.

- Never stop by a company to set up a meeting, even if you already know the person!

- Meetings should be no longer than 20 to 30 minutes.

How to Schedule the Meeting:

Here is the language you can use to get people to open your email, text, letter, or answer your phone call. Keep in mind that it is your responsibility to follow up with a call, text, or email to schedule the meeting. If you contact the person via phone, it's up to you to request the meeting. Here are some helpful tips for crafting an effective message:

- Use the "I am …" statement you have developed.

- Include that you are "seeking to learn more about your company, product, or service …"

- Include the name of the person who referred you and share what you discussed in 10 words or less.

- Mention that "they said you would be a valuable source of information on this topic."

- Say, "I welcome the opportunity to meet with you."

- Provide two to three sentences outlining your background. Be sure they are on point with the topic to be discussed.

- Close with "I will contact you on_____to schedule a convenient time to talk." (You must follow up!)

The Actual Face-to-Face Meeting (includes video conferencing meetings):

First Impressions Matter!

- Be on time! Arriving on-site for a 9:00 am meeting at 9:00 am is too late. Instead, arrive 5–10 minutes early. (If using conferencing technology, ensure it works before the meeting.)

- Dress professionally. Be clean and neat. (Yes, this is true even when you're not physically meeting face to face.)

- Avoid distracting background art and noises.

- Don't chew gum.

- To help connect with the person faster, wear a tie/scarf, suit, or shirt/blouse that matches your eye color.

- Always be nice to the receptionist, assistant, or server at the restaurant or coffee shop where you meet.

- Shake hands and provide a business card.

- Do not leave your brochure, web link, video, or other marketing/sales item.

The Actual Meeting: Getting Off on the Right Foot

- Introduce yourself by clearly stating your first and last names.

- Extend your hand for a handshake.

- Be sure you're looking them in the eyes.

- Make a statement about the person who introduced you by stating that person's full name and adding that "they said that you would be a valuable source of information." This sentence opens up many reticent individuals who do not want to meet with you!

The Actual Meeting: The Meeting!

Since you are trying to establish a good relationship with this person, keep the conversation positive and your tone of voice neutral. It's up to you to guide the meeting forward by setting up the purpose of the meeting and keeping it focused.

- Thank them for meeting with you.

- Restate the full name of the person who referred you.

- Add "They said you would be a valuable source of information." (Yes, this is an intentional repeat.)

- Reiterate the time frame for the meeting: "As I shared when setting up this meeting, I plan on taking about 20 to 30 minutes and have specific questions to ask."

- Remind them you are here to learn more about their industry, profession, and company.

- Set the tone. Share your "I am …" and "My background includes …" statements. This sets the context for a business meeting.

Most salespeople, business owners, and consultants make huge mistakes by assuming they know how a company operates. Always have good business questions ready, regardless of whether you've worked for this company, boss, or team members or have done business with a similar company in the past. Perspectives and business practices change with new bosses and employees over time. Ask questions, probe, and openly listen to the responses without judgment.

Write your questions down and take the list with you. Use a conversational tone, this is not an interrogation. Some ideas to get you started:

- What type of challenges has the company experienced? (Be sure you've done your online and network investigation.)

- Are they aware of what started the issue?

- What do they believe are the solutions?

- What results did they achieve when they implemented these solutions?

- What do they believe is the next logical step?

- What do they believe could be a challenge or limitation with the next step?

Keep in mind that confidentiality is important.

Do not lose control or focus, or the other person may turn the networking meeting into a yes or no meeting.

The Actual Meeting: Summary

- Although your research before your meeting should have prepared you for key issues, it's important to recap the top three issues discussed and your background in those areas and how you've addressed them—don't forget to include your numbers! Remember, the key issues may be different than anticipated. Remember, brevity is critical!

- Ask, "How can I help you?"

The Actual Meeting: Asking for Referrals

Ask who they would recommend that you speak with next:

- "Of the people you are professionally or personally associated with, who would you recommend I talk with further about _____?"

- "Could you suggest other people you are professionally associated with who would be willing to talk to me about _____?"

(Note: Be aware of just being given a name and contact information—the referred person is not likely to respond or meet with you. Instead, request the person you are meeting with to send an introductory email to you and the referred person. This will increase the likelihood that the referred person will respond to you. Social media introductions can easily be overlooked since many busy people don't check these sites often.)

The Actual Meeting: End of Meeting (On-site)

- Thank them for their time.

- Shake hands and exit.

- Do NOT leave brochures or other written materials unless specifically requested.

- Do leave a business card.

After the Meeting

The biggest challenge for most people after networking meetings is following up and following through. Outline with the other person what you will provide them and when you will do so. Then, call to ensure they received the information and determine the next step. Developing positive relationships is essential. Many base their future interactions on the person's ability to do what they say they will do. It also will make a difference when it comes time to close the sale.

- Send the person a thank you email, text, letter, or card within 24 hours.

- Remember, the #1 and #2 reasons people fail to buy from you is because you didn't follow up and follow through! Get it done immediately!

- Include any information that you promised to provide.

- Send a thank you to the person who referred you.

The person who referred you may have additional contacts for you to talk with and will be glad you followed up on their suggestions.

Review – Part I (Immediately Afterwards)

Write down or note on your CRM (customer relationship management system) the following (do not rely on your memory):

- Who did I talk with: name, title, background, company?

- What did I learn about the department, company, industry, profession, issues, company, or industry jargon?

- What are the problems and issues for the company, department, industry, or profession?

- What are possible solutions?

- How does this align with my company's purpose, interests, and expertise?

- Who can I refer this person to if my company doesn't handle those interests or doesn't have that expertise? (Send an introductory email to set up a conversation after you've received permission from both parties.)

Review – Part II (After 24 Hours)

Consider the following questions. I find it helps to write down my thoughts.

- What changes do I need to make in my presentation?

- Am I asking the right questions?

- Am I getting the type of information I need?

- Am I being referred to the right people? If not, whom do I talk with?

- Do I need to update my "I am …" and "My background includes …" statements?

Do

- Be prepared with an agenda

- Treat this as an important meeting

- Ask and expect referrals

- Actively listen

- Be coachable if asking for advice on a professional or personal matter

- Practice, practice, practice before each meeting

- Determine a weekly goal of meetings and follow through

- Update your social media sites (e.g., LinkedIn, Facebook, etc.) weekly with positive comments (do not include the names of people you met with unless there is mutual agreement to do so)

Don't

- Fall into "they interview you" trap due to being unprepared

- Leave behind a brochure or other unrequested written information (this cannot be said often enough; you are building a relationship, and it requires you to talk and communicate effectively)

- Get defensive

- Get into political or religious discussions

- Vent your frustrations

- Post information about your meeting with the person on social media

- Change your goals to meet your results. (Note: Frequently pivoting or changing your focus point won't help you attract new clients or interests.)

- Post inappropriate comments on your social media sites

- Conduct meetings with high-level decision-makers without having conducted at least three other networking meetings previously with people who can tell you about the person and their company, business practices, and internal challenges

Whether you are starting a new job, in a new profession, or have advanced in your career, making and taking the time to network is critical. It's essential to develop and keep meaningful relationships. You never know when things may change, and you may need to reach out for help—or others may need to tap you on the shoulder for help.

To meet the right people and keep your network viable, make the time to meet and expand the types of people you engage with and the types of events you attend.

The key is to keep your network alive and well. Following up and following through are two of the most important steps. Networking works when you stay in touch with others and are available if they need anything. If you only contact your network when you need something, people will stop helping you!

Effective networking means you can work smarter, not harder. Often, people who effectively conduct networking meetings enjoy it. Beware of the trap of confusing lots of activity with achieving your intended result: closing your next sale, winning an award, or getting to the right decision-maker.

Questions to Ask Yourself:

- Are you getting the types of introductions that fit your goals?

- Are you getting closer to meeting the right decision-maker(s)?

- Are you getting closer to finding new opportunities? If not, what do you need to transform?

(Note: Consider that it could be your attitude or belief about yourself and others if you're not getting the type of information or contacts you need.)

- Talk with your coach, mentor, or friend for insights. We all have blind spots. It takes someone else's insight to help us see more clearly.

11

Close the Sale

"Stop leaving money on the table!"
—Jeannette Seibly

We've been talking about networking and marketing yourself and your company in a positive way to establish credibility upfront. These efforts significantly affect your ability to compete for the sale. Now it's time to use your brag material to help you close the sale, win the award, or receive the contract bid.

When writing out a draft of your accomplishments for a sales presentation, an award nomination, or a contract bid, use your KTAs as the outline. You can also complete separate KTAs (lists of achievements with numbers) for the team, company, and product/service when they are being mentioned. From there, include the other information required by the RFP, RFQ, industry, or company in their submission instructions. When answering these questions, use your brag statements. For example, if the question is "How many times have you _____?", a potential answer might be "In the past xx years, we have handled yy projects resulting in $zz in sales."

Company and industry awards may be internally driven and subjective. Be sure to let your boss know verbally and in writing of your achievements after each project. He or she can often provide additional information or contacts to help you better understand the process and what information will make the difference in vying for the award. For internal recognition, a boss or company mentor can provide insights into office politics and additional resources that may be required to support you and your team in achieving the goal. Many times, awards are based on how well a submission is written. Be sure to have it professionally reviewed and edited before sending it in. And don't forget to include your brags using numbers!

Remember to appropriately include any networking information (aka information gleaned from your networking meetings) to address any concerns, along with your metrics and accomplishments. If you don't win the sale or the award, call the decision-maker to clarify what was missing in your submission or presentation and include this information in the future.

When preparing your sales presentation or speech introduction, outline your brag statements. Then include your "I am …" and "My background includes …" statements to share in your introduction and periodically throughout your talk. Don't forget to include your numbers and other metrics! Remember to keep the message short and on point, usually one to three paragraphs. Long-winded introductions rarely make a good impression, build credibility, or hold people's attention.

LinkedIn and Social Media Venues

Use this process to create brag statements for you and your books, products, or services. Share them on your social media venues, particularly on LinkedIn.

Check out mine at *https://www.linkedin.com/in/jeannetteseibly/*

12

Attracting New Clients

"People want to work with winners."
—Jeannette Seibly

Being referred to a decision-maker by a networking source can make the process easier. First, the decision-maker will review your online presence before they talk with you. Be sure they are wowed by what they read by using your brag statements and the information provided by the person introducing you. If you are offering the referral, I find introducing both parties in an email to be a great practice and include one brag about each person. Then, let them connect with each other.

Another method is to invite them both to coffee or lunch (or conference video) and provide an introduction at that time (include a link for their background information using their website and LinkedIn profile). If you are the referral recipient, when you receive these types of emails, respond quickly and don't attempt to sell at this time by providing marketing slogans and content. People readily make "yes" or "no" decisions based on the "sales copy" and it's usually a "no."

When setting up meetings, be flexible and meet where it is most convenient for the potential client. During the meeting, narrow down the top reasons you can help them and stay focused. Trying to provide too much too soon with too many possibilities usually ends with the potential client postponing their decision to work with you, then, after a period of time, deciding not to move forward with you. Remember to keep it simple and smart when providing quotes and proposals.

Keep Straying Clients

If you have a straying client, prepare a list of all the activities and results you've provided to the company or your contact. Be sure to use your KTAs as an outline. If you are a sales representative, consultant, or business owner, share them when renewing contracts or looking to increase your sales through upselling or cross-selling. Most clients are unaware of what you have done for them, the money you've saved them, and the results achieved. By using this method, several of my clients have held on to large clients who were being wooed by the competition.

I had a recent experience where someone was defensive about her work when questioned about the amount of time she was taking to get a project done. She sent back several long emails stating she was the best at what she did and that her time commitment was better than others.

These types of emails, conversations, or texts are not bragging in a business savvy manner. This is why people are called braggarts—when they compare themselves to others. While you may initially keep the client, chances are they will look elsewhere in the future.

- *Do not defend.*

- *Do not compare.*

- *Simply state what you've done using your numbers. (KTAs)*

- *This goes a long way towards keeping a client.*

Group and Company Brags

Don't forget another great idea (mentioned in Chapter 8, Practice, Practice, Practice) of using the brag method within your department, team, or business unit. What have you achieved as a group? What are your unique qualities or areas of expertise? Exploring these questions is a great way to build team loyalty and share the knowledge and information your team can provide. Remember, it starts with each person completing their own KTAs and then combining them. It's also a great reminder of the successful results you've had with a client who may be considering a move to your competition. When creating an employer brand to attract new employees, doing your KTAs is important.

13

Nominations/Contract Bids

"When you take the time to do the work, it shows. You're often rewarded!"
—Jeannette Seibly

To win nominations for awards or submit RFQ/RFP (Request for Quotation or Request for Proposal), requires your brags! Numbers often and quickly convey your qualifications. While many people have a reluctance to use their numbers due to being afraid of numbers—remember, it's not rocket science—it's simply how companies keep score.[4] These will differentiate you, your company, and product/service from others. Remember to answer all the questions directly or provide information that addresses every one of the criteria.

Outline:

- Get submission requirements and be sure you or your company meet them.

- Complete your KTAs on you, your product/service, company, and other requirements.

---

[4] Knight, Rebecca, "How to Improve Your Finance Skills (Even If You Hate Numbers)," *Harvard Business Review,* https://hbr.org/2017/03/how-to-improve-your-finance-skills-even-if-you-hate-numbers, March 31, 2017.

- Talk with your network about what the award committee or company is really seeking (any unwritten considerations).

- When possible, get a copy of someone else's submission as an example. Do NOT plagiarize.

- Write a draft.
  - For nominations, they often want a story. Incorporate your "brags" along the way.

  - For RFQs/RFPs it's critical that you use brags (numbers, metrics, and facts) when talking about your product/service and yourself/company.

- Have someone review your documents to see what may be missing.

- Submit all paperwork by the deadline, preferably a day early to avoid any snafus.

I've talked with several people and groups that fail to use their brags, numbers, metrics, and other facts for grants. "Oh, we don't do it that way." Nine times out of ten they also don't receive the money or funding required for their good cause.

One new business owner called me for coaching. She wanted to win a contract with a large utility. After doing the Brag! work, she was awarded a million-dollar contract, and her business grew. Also, she used her brags for professional recognition as a fast-growing business in her industry.

14

Negotiate

"You can expand your results by ensuring win-win-win results through good negotiation skills."
—Jeannette Seibly

Have you ever talked with someone and created a new idea, project, or solution?

But failed to negotiate and document the conversation?

Then, later, you found out they didn't agree to everything you remember them agreeing to?

This happens frequently. Why? People rely on their memories … and memories are often faulty or selective, or they change their minds without considering the impact.

There will be times when you need to negotiate closing a sale or accepting a contract and ensuring price, terms, and other specific requirements are specified to fulfill the agreement.

You can create win-win-win results by using your brag statements and the information gleaned from networking to support your requests.

Steps Required for Effective Negotiation

It starts with a clear mindset:

Rule #1 — Prepare.

- Be clear about your goals or end results required. Write them down!

- Don't settle for the minimum.

- Clarify your intentions or write down three "Must-Have" outcomes. If you have a long laundry list of requirements, a potential new customer or business partner will move on.

- Ensure the contract provides a positive return on investment (ROI) in addition to generating money for you and your company.

How to Create Your Three "Must-Have" Outcomes. Write down everything you'd ideally want to achieve. Then, rank order. Review the top ten items and review—this includes reordering and rewriting. Then, circle the top three. These are your three "Must-Haves." Keep them where you can easily find them! And, don't overlook them during the negotiation process—this can be easy to do when you get excited about the new idea or other possibilities.

Rule #2 — Research the other party's interests and potential objections.

- Learn as much about the other person(s), company, and their goals and challenges. Using the Networking Works process (SEE Chapter 10, Networking Works) learn as much as you can from your network.

For example: Conducting an AI training program when the company is going through layoffs may not be a good idea. Have clarity about "why" this is important to them at this time, and make sure there is buy-in from the top and middle management. Negotiations should include payment, delay in delivering the program, and key points and outcomes required (which may be different than originally agreed upon).

Rule #3 — Be prepared to walk away. What is your bottom line?

It's critical (really, it's crucial) that you are willing to walk away if there isn't a win-win-win outcome. This requires knowing your numbers and other business metrics! Being emotionally attached to the results (e.g., working with a specific person, getting a $100K contract) can make you regret winning the contract when those conditions don't materialize.

The Meeting: If you've completed your requirements with regards to Rules 1, 2, and 3 (you've written this all down), you're ready for your first negotiation (or negotiating) meeting.

During the Discussions:

- **Be Present.** This practice of mindfulness is crucial for achieving the desired outcomes. (SEE Chapter 20, Mindfulness Keeps You Moving Forward) By being fully present, you can avoid the risk of agreeing to something you don't recall later on, a common pitfall in negotiations.

(Note: Today, there are many memory challenges due to COVID, working baby boomers, an increase in mental health challenges, and people who multi-task instead of listening. These can lead to false memories too. If this happens during the conversation, paint a picture of what you remember by describing where you both met and any unusual situation (the coffee shop didn't sell tea). Stay factual.)

Also, remember, if you have previously worked with the person, team, and/ or company—needs change! Goals change. People change. These changes will impact conversations and situations since perspectives have changed too. Be flexible, open to learning, and take responsibility for ensuring what you're offering is a good fit. *Learn to ask open-ended questions and not assume!* (SEE: Learn to Ask Open-Ended Questions, on next page)

- **Use an Agenda!** Agendas facilitate keeping the conversation on point. They also help make note-taking easier and they serve as a future reminder for action items and a to-do list.

- **Take notes!** People overlook the importance of getting everyone on the same page, closing sales, and building good working relationships, especially in negotiations. Use whatever materials are at hand including paper or your cell phone to take notes—and keep these in a folder even after the agreement and project have been completed. Then, immediately, memorialize in an email, text, and/or letter and outline points of agreement. This includes noting dates and times. Also, include points of disagreement, other concerns, and opportunities not yet discussed. Ask the other party to review and make any changes as soon as possible. Go back and forth until both parties are satisfied.

- **Let them talk first!** This strategic step will provide you with needed information and insights before offering your perspectives, products/services, and requirements.

- **Listen!** This is not a time to multi-task. Put away your electronics and listen. There are times when the other party will not be 100% on board. Don't ignore their position. Instead, ask them "why" and other open-ended questions. (SEE below: Learn to Ask Open-Ended Questions)

  - During the conversation, discuss priorities and desired outcomes. Write them down!
  - Address any misunderstandings or misconceptions.
  - Explore creative solutions that benefit both sides.
  - Be flexible and willing to compromise.
  - Look for mutually beneficial trade-offs.
  - Avoid adversarial tactics.
  - Listen. Listen. Listen!

  Here's an example: If you're working with a commercial leasing agent and they are doing a build-out of the space for you, be clear as to your specs. Let's say you need an additional bathroom in the office area, write it down. Ask, "Where would the bathroom be located? This is why it's important." Then, note who will talk with the plumber, pull a building permit (if required), and/or speak with the city code enforcer. "All this will be done by what date?"

- **Learn to Ask Open-Ended Questions:** Never assume you know what the other person(s) means. When you ask open-ended questions, it invites and encourages better conversations and positive interactions. Then, use their responses proactively! This skill is critical to discovering the solutions and ideas needed to resolve problems and move forward for win-win-win results.

The challenge is we're not wired to ask open-ended questions and this limits our results. When you use open-ended questions and have at least three questions ready to get and keep the other person(s) talking, it's amazing what you can learn and the new ideas that are generated, especially when the team or conversation is stuck (e.g., circular logic, same-old excuses).

What are open-ended questions?

- Cannot be answered with a yes or no
- Cannot be answered with one-word responses
- Do not have pre-defined answers
- Allows others to provide insights that have not been considered
- Promotes in-depth discussions
- Energizes conversations and meetings

How to begin asking open-ended questions:

Start with: Who, What, When, Where, Why, and How type questions. Using these words at the beginning of a question will open up opportunities for others to respond.

Examples:

- Who should be involved, and why?
- What are the hidden costs of this idea?
- When is a good time to start, and why?

- Where are good places to host this event?
- Why is this important?
- How do you propose we move forward?

Other ways to start open-ended questions:

- Tell me about …
- Please describe …
- I'm interested in learning more …

Other considerations:

- **Seek common ground.** After a person has made the point, restate using the same words to ensure you're both on the same page. (Example: Use the same word of generous and don't use a different synonym, magnanimous, which most people don't know.) Then, build on areas of agreement before moving on to other points or interjecting new ideas.

- **Review.** At the end of each conversation, don't forget to come back and review all the points and agreements made—and note any changes made during the course of the conversation. These can impact, change, or negate previous agreements. Remember, everyone makes their own assumptions and interpretations. While we all think we have great memories, the truth is we don't.

- **Don't gloss over details.** These can be deal-breakers if not addressed!

- **Don't dismiss concerns** by stating, "It's not important."

- **Don't avoid talking about any elephants in the room!** (Example: When negotiating a contract to sell assessments. "What are the results you need to achieve?" How will these be used (e.g., hiring, coaching, training, managing)?" "Who do I invoice?" "When will payment be received?" "What type of training is required?")

- **Allow for Silence and Don't Talk Over Anyone.** Stay focused on the topic. Remember, being dismissive, joking, or minimizing a detail can (and will) haunt the agreement and hurt your ability to work together in the future.

- **Talk Straight and Don't Hedge.** Don't say, "Maybe we can talk about it later." If it's an important issue, talk about it now. Or schedule time to complete the conversation.

Finalize Agreement:

- Reach an agreement on terms and conditions.

- Document the agreement in writing.

- Ensure clarity regarding responsibilities and timelines.

- Consider involving legal experts to ensure the agreement is enforceable.

- Have an "escape clause" or "back-door" if things change, or if you or the other party have a lot of excuses, or the person is no longer interested.

- Again, do NOT say, "We'll address it later." Too often these are deal breakers and memories will often conflict after time, money, and energy have been spent.

- Review notes made during and after each meeting. Keep all notes in the same file, making them easier to find later. Include date and time. Be specific to ensure accuracy and win-win-win outcomes. This makes it easier when it's time to create a legal agreement or determine if and when you're ready to launch a new project.

Start Project: Implementation and Execution

- Do not begin work until all parties have signed the agreement.

- Get part of the money upfront, as per the contract.

- Execute the agreed-upon terms.

- Monitor progress and address any issues.

- Maintain a positive relationship with the other party.

- Be flexible and responsible for honoring the agreement.

- Remember to talk out any discrepancies as soon as possible.

- People will forget the "why." Don't be shy about sharing your brags and stories similar to the challenge or lack of motivation—these are normal!

- Learn from the negotiation experience for future improvements.

Negotiation is about finding common ground, building relationships, and achieving mutually beneficial outcomes. It's a win-win-win all the way!

15

Pitching Your Products/ Services/Books/Ideas

"You must know your numbers and business metrics when offering ideas or solutions! Or, risk being ignored or working for free."
—Jeannette Seibly

This chapter focuses on pitching your ideas, books, products, and services.

Examples:

- Talking with an event planner about being a keynote speaker or conducting a workshop for a conference.

- Offering an idea to a current or prospective client.

- Selling your book at an event.

(Note: If you're seeking an investor or large product buyer, it would be best to do an online search for "pitching" and learn the preliminary information, then, network with others who have successfully pitched at that level since millions of dollars are normally at stake. Don't forget to include your KTAs.)

Six Step Process:

1. What is your goal? Be specific. (The more specific you are the easier it will be to create your pitch.) Keep it short, ten words or less.

2. Complete your KTAs on the product/service/book/idea.

3. Address these questions before moving forward:
   - Who's the audience or buyer?
     - Reader
     - Company
     - HR, IT, or another manager
     - Bookstore
     - Event audience (e.g., business owners, entrepreneurs, investors, engineers, bookstore buyers)
   - What is it that you are selling or sharing?
     - Presentation or Keynote
     - Assessments for hiring, coaching, or training
     - Technology services (e.g., AI, website, app)
     - Books
   - When is the product/service/idea/book available?
     - Now or later or as soon as an agreement is signed (be specific)
   - Where can it be purchased or taken?
     - You or your company or employer
   - Why is it important?
     - Spend time and ensure you're including the KTAs
     - **Numbers are critical** (e.g., Increase in retention and reduction in turnover, decrease in call-outs for HVAC,

losing weight with a trainer, taking a supplement to reduce cholesterol)

- What are they going to learn? Enjoy?
- How is it going to help them succeed, feel good, or make money?
- How can it make their lives easier and more fun?

4. Now, write your script in a way that captures the audience's or gatekeeper's attention (e.g., event planner):

- Start with an attention-grabbing statement or question. This requires being clear about the theme of your book or the purpose of your idea, product, or service.

Examples to get you started:

a. If you write young adult dragon books, start by asking, "Do you like dragons?" Don't start by telling the potential reader about writing the book for your grandchildren. (They don't care and you've lost their interest.)

b. If you want to sell human resources, technology, marketing, or other consulting services, "Do you experience costly turnover?" OR, "Did you know AI can reduce time in writing and sending emails?"

c. If you sell cosmetics or supplements: "Would you like to reduce the time you spend getting ready for work?"

d. Getting the attention of an event planner or bookstore: "This book is an International Amazon Bestseller and I was awarded best speaker at the ABC conference."

- Problem Statement: Clearly articulate the problem or need your idea/product/service addresses.

  Examples to get you started:

  a. (Keeping with the dragon theme above—remember the age of the reader/buyer): "I collected 30 dragons during my career in the navy—at each port I would buy a dragon." Keep it short! Use a number or two! OR—"Jacob's sword was magical and the dragon was his best friend as they fought the bad wizard and won."

  b. (Consulting services): "I've helped more than 30 companies reduce the cost of turnover by more than $250,000—some of these companies had turnover of more than 100%!"

  c. "More than 25 of my clients have reduced their cholesterol by 10 points. They have more energy, mentally and physically."

- Briefly introduce yourself and your background.

  a. Use your "I am…" statement.

  b. ONLY if they ask for you to tell them more, share one paragraph of your "My background includes …"

5. Share information from networking, the purpose of the book or idea, and the internet:

- Explain with brevity the gaps or opportunities gleaned through your research. Again, USE NUMBERS, FACTS, METRICS. Have your sources available.

- Describe your target audience, niche, or customer segment.

- Briefly highlight solutions and how your solution made a difference (again, numbers and metrics are essential). Brevity is key! Don't overwhelm them. Only cite one or two stats or numbers to grab their attention.

6. Close:

- Tell them what you've told them

- Remind them "What's in it for them"

- Let them know how you see this working for them

- Ask if there are questions

- Wrap up with a brag about the results you achieved for another client

Key Factors to Remember:

- Stay out of "how" your product/service/idea/book works. Or, "how" you created it.

- Do NOT bore them with product/service/book/idea details at this point or they will no longer be interested. But it's critical that you know the details when asked a direct question. If a demonstration is required, set one up.

- Note: Use a Non-Disclosure Agreement (NDA) if this is a new book idea, or new product or service you want to roll out to a company or potential buyer/investor/partner. When you fail to use a NDA, the other person or company may create a similar competitive product. (I've seen it happen.)

- Follow-up and follow-through. Provide information requested (e.g., send Speaker Bio to event planner, link to buy book, product brochure, and other requested information to company buyer).

- Keep it simple. This is so critical! I cannot say it enough. If you are long-winded and have not done your "brag" work about yourself, the company, and the product/service/idea/book, you will lose their attention.

- Include brief "brags" about you, the company, and the people delivering the product or service.

- If appropriate, provide a timeline with milestones (keep action steps general until later—during the negotiation phase).

When pitching, the goal is to get the prospective buyer to agree and sign a contract. Remember, getting to a "yes" can take time and persistence. Don't make the mistake of disappearing if the prospect says no.

16

Business or Career Transitions

"How you communicate your brags will determine your next opportunities."
—Jeannette Seibly

Changing professions, industries, or retiring to become a consultant or coach creates the need to develop "what's next?" Too often, executives downplay their skills, interests, and talents since they didn't need to do so when they relied on their job title or position to communicate who they were.

The bad news is, today, it matters less and less what someone's job title is or was. What's important is what they have achieved (brags), the results produced (brags), and how they can help others achieve the same or similar results (brags).

- First, complete your KTAs.

- Second, dial up the humility and dial down the ego. (I've seen too many executives allow their egos to get in the way when endeavoring to create their next career or opportunity.)

- Third, develop a can-do attitude and be open.

- Fourth, mindfulness and being present when talking with others is critical. Again, set aside the ego! Going from an executive where everything was done for you to being an entrepreneur means you need to pay for those same services or do them yourself!

Build on your experience to date:

1. Update your brag statements and do the work outlined earlier in this *Get Your Brag On!* book. (SEE Chapters 5, Steps One, Two, Three: KTAs (Knowledge, Talents, Achievements); Chapter 6, Step Four: I Am; Chapter 7, Step Five: My Background Includes)

2. Learn how to network for clarity about what a specific company, industry, or profession is seeking. (SEE Chapter 10, Networking Works)

3. Be open and prepared to share those specifics when interviewing for a job or seeking new clients as a consultant, coach, or sales rep.

Lorie bought and sold five companies during her 20-year career. Now, she wanted to join her husband and sell an identity theft plan to prevent hackers from stealing people's identities.

My advice was to start with completing the brag statements and clarifying who she had the most interaction with during her 20 years as a business owner and investor.

Then, focus on selling (at least initially) to these people (e.g., business owners, specific vendors, suppliers, former clients, etc.) and use the "I am a former business owner who has transitioned into saving millions of people their identity." (one example of using a brag statement)

17

Get Your Ideas Heard

**"Sharing your ideas and having them heard
is empowering to you and others."**
—Jeannette Seibly

Ideas create a kernel or possibility to build solutions, generate new business growth, and improve and expand working relationships. However, it requires you to stand up and speak up.

"But wait,"—you may exclaim!

Your "Yeah, buts" are why your ideas are not being offered, heard, or acted upon.

Here are the secrets to getting your ideas heard and valued!

- First, understand why your team members and leaders don't listen to you.

- Second, share your ideas so that others will listen to you using your brags.

- Third, flexibility is required without losing the purpose/goal crucial for success.

- Fourth, include your brags as inspiration along the way.

Why Are Your Ideas Not Heard?

Ego. Underneath all the excuses, either your ego or the other person's ego is in the way. This could be due to arrogance, righteousness, or skepticism. If you encounter someone's resistance to change, give it time and repeat it later.

You're Not Listening! If you fail to listen to others' concerns, fears, or rebuttals, they will refuse to listen to you.

First Time They Are Hearing It. You've been thinking about your idea for a while; give others time to catch up! Don't be afraid of repeating the idea at another time.

Be Aware of Different Thinking Styles. Some people learn aurally. Some people learn visually. Some people learn by doing. Left and right brain types approach information differently. There are many different styles of learning. Keep the details to a minimum when creating a big picture, and be prepared to answer specific questions for those that learn point-by-point. People absorb new information at different rates of speed. Be clear and brief, and prepared to repeat.

Ask Open-Ended Questions. "Yes" or "no" questions generally result in a no. Instead, ask open-ended questions and encourage the other person(s) to share their thoughts. Otherwise, your idea will be dead before it can move forward.

Lack of Empowerment. Many people feel disempowered to take new ideas and explore them. Be clear that you are open to their input. Encourage, listen, and build on what they say (especially if it's an off-the-wall idea). These are usually the best ways to move ideas forward.

How to Present Ideas So Others Hear You

Presenting Your Ideas. Do your research, learn the facts (not false information), and logically outline your discussion points to make it easier for others to follow. Don't be shy about addressing elephants in the room but be responsible for how you choose to do so (e.g., with fun, or compassion, and respectfully).

Choose Your Words Responsibly. Keep it simple. Remember, team members will shut down if you rely on jargon, slang, or acronyms. Or it could be using the "F" word. If others continually ask you for clarification, you've lost them, and they've stopped listening to your idea(s). Stop. Get coaching. Do it again at a later time.

Use Fact-Based versus Emotional Messaging. If you usually use one or the other, expand. For example, if you rely on "emotional messages" to get people's attention, share facts and be a contrarian.

Example:

- Start with a contrarian statement: *Did you know intuitive hiring is how many companies hire and is one of the leading causes of job dissatisfaction?*
- Then, follow up with a couple of quick facts. *Studies have shown that more than 90% of hiring is based solely on interviews. And "yes" or "no" decisions are made within the first 4 to 15 minutes. There is a lack of objective data collected for making selection decisions.*

- Now, the emotional message of 'why it's important.' *This way of hiring is costly due to the failure to obtain objective data and needs to be changed to improve our bottom line and bonuses.* (Note: Refer to my book: *Hire Amazing Employees: How to Increase Retention, Revenues and Results!*)

Use Graphics and Pictures. To get everyone on the same page, convey your ideas using easy-to-understand graphics and pictures. You can also physically show them the issue and how your idea will solve it.

Do Mirror Work. Practice your presentation in front of the mirror using your outline. Do this in various ways (e.g., humorous, emotionally charged, serious) to develop your ability to feel comfortable in each situation. You can also do this with family, friends, and business associates.

Be Open to Others' Ideas. Listen and build on them. Remember, listening is a two-way street. Allow others to offer their ideas to create a workable solution that they consider a win-win-win. Now, build on your original idea incorporating their input. Share the credit!

Remember, remember, remember, to incorporate your brags along the way of how the idea worked for you in the past.

18

Invaluable Career Wisdom

**"Your attitude is an asset or a liability.
It's your choice."**
—Jeannette Seibly

Commitment is the key to success in any career, business group, or entrepreneurial venture. Too often, we say we're committed to something; however, when we don't follow through, attend meetings on time, or engage with others effectively, people question our commitment—even when we have the best excuses!

A lack of commitment, for whatever reason, makes people question the quality of your ideas, books, products, and services and whether you are someone they want to do business with or partner with. (Regardless of your great brags.)

Even if you believe you have the commitment, if you don't have a can-do attitude, you will struggle to attract the right prospects and close sales.

A positive attitude influences your sales, industry, or professional recognition and career options, now and in the future. It's why some people get introductions to others' networks or are invited to present their products and services, even though they have fewer qualifications than you.

Brag statements, networking, and building credibility are important skills to develop if you want to have a satisfying career and develop professionally over your lifetime. They are great reflections of a positive and confident attitude when you share them.

For people who are self-employed, independent contractors, or in sales, it can take a lot of work to stay positive and do the required work daily. In Chapter 20, Mindfulness Keeps You Moving Forward, you'll find exercises to keep your mindset positive, especially after a setback or bad day or week. These exercises can be easily done between meetings, at the end of the day, week, or month, or on an as-needed basis. In addition, on the next couple of pages, you'll find some tips to maintain your image as an influential business professional.

Luck Is Preparation!

As a successful business professional, consultant, author, or executive, it's always important to be prepared and develop the technical, financial, sales, management, and project skills required, even if you need to pay for the courses, workshops, or books yourself.

Some opportunities may only appear once! After a while, they will stop if you are not ready and willing to do the work required. Stop blaming others and take responsibility for developing the right skills, and use them! People want to work with winners to solve their challenges or concerns.

Additional Items for You to Consider:

- Keep financial debt to a minimum (preferably, have none). Too often, opportunities come along that people cannot take advantage of because they can't afford it.

- Keep your credit scores high and keep your credit report clean. Some businesses run financial checks before doing business with you. Use a mainstream identity theft company to keep track of your credit, banking, passwords, and other important information.

- Take time to learn new skills (e.g., software, Internet, music, jigsaw puzzles, gardening, public speaking, writing, negotiating, publishing). Share about your experiences on your social media sites.

- Develop yourself professionally and personally by learning to elicit the best in yourself and others and work through limiting beliefs you have about others and producing intended results.

When you attend an event that becomes life-changing for you, don't immediately buy into the concept or attempt to adopt it as your own. What works for one person may not work or be appropriate for you. For example, adopting the "F" word has become common by some presenters. This is actually offensive in many companies. I heard of one fast-rising employee in a company mimicking the "F" word said at a board meeting—the person was later sidelined and didn't know why.

Take away one or two insights from these experiences and create a structure for fulfilling the new skills given to you. Work with your boss, executive coach, and an industry mentor to ensure you use and build on these insights appropriately.

- Remember, developing self-confidence by self-promoting encourages others to share what their companies are really needing and looking for with you.

- Use brag statements to communicate your achievements to help others feel more comfortable talking with you. Failure to do so can result in people not feeling comfortable with you, especially if you downplay your skills.

- Don't stretch the truth. Answer the prospective client's questions appropriately and honestly using your brag statements. Don't respond with what you think they want to hear. In addition, learn to ask open-ended questions for clarification. Otherwise, you will often be wrong in your assumptions. Major career derailment happens if you make a sale and your customers feel scammed. Having a client say, "There is nothing worse than working with a liar!" hurts your ability to get new clients.

- Take time to reassess your life goals periodically. Life does change, and so can your goals, personal and professional needs, and aspirations.

- Know your strengths and weaknesses since truly understanding yourself gives you a competitive edge. Use a qualified assessment to help you clarify them and learn who you are based on objective data, not who you want to be seen as. Go to https://SeibCo.com/contact/ to learn more about what a qualified assessment is and why using one is important.

- Don't be a lone ranger. Ask for help. Be willing to accept help graciously.

- Make it a habit to send thank you notes or cards!

- Hire an experienced executive coach outside your business and find an inside mentor in your industry. Issues that people often discuss with a coach include being more effective, communication skills, developing business and professional savvy, and developing confidence. In addition, having a confidential sounding board to bounce off ideas and to brainstorm how to handle problems with motivating the team can be very helpful. Meet regularly with an industry mentor to stay up-to-date on any industry, profession, and potential company changes.

- Get involved in and attend trade or professional association meetings. Be sure that your efforts are in alignment with the type of client you can help. For example, attending a mergers and acquisitions meeting may be interesting; however, if you and/or your company don't provide those types of services, it's taking your time away from meeting the right people in groups where your expertise is wanted and where potential sales abound.

- Life has a way of getting our attention, particularly when we don't want to listen. When you experience challenges with bosses, employees, clients, or if you are bored or unwilling to do your job, hire a coach or therapist. Find out why now, before it's too late to get help with your career choice.

- Respect all people you meet and their opinions and feelings. You can achieve this by listening more than talking, maintaining confidentiality, returning all phone calls within 24 to 48 hours, keeping your commitments and following up quickly, dressing for success, arriving at least five minutes early for each meeting, posting appropriate messages on your social media sites, and having a professionally scripted voicemail message.

- Remember, companies select vendors and suppliers for their reasons, not yours. You cannot sell unless you understand their needs. Do not burn bridges by telling current or future clients they were wrong to offer the contract to someone else. Stay in touch. If it was the wrong vendor, they may call you soon.

- Always, always, always go to a meeting prepared. It doesn't take that much time to go online to find and read the company's name and products and services and other information. The most significant error is when salespeople or business consultants believe they understand an organization's culture, issues, and possible solutions, especially if they've never worked for the company. Learn to ask open-ended questions, listen, and not be seen as a "know-it-all."

- Stop trying to be a mind reader or tell people how they feel. Too often, we take the tiniest bits of information and believe we know what the person is trying to say or feel and add our own meaning to it. You will almost always be wrong, and people will not feel heard. You will lose out on professional opportunities, obtaining critical information, and being offered leads or other needed support to be successful.

The bottom line is this: Stop waiting for the perfect time or the opportunities will diminish. Learn how to brag! Showcase your confidence and credentials by effectively using your brag statements when networking, presenting, and writing. Achieving industry or professional recognition isn't that hard when you've learned how to brag in a business-savvy manner.

Keep your copy of *Get Your Brag On!* and update your brag statements in the KTA worksheets (blank worksheets found at the back of this book) periodically to keep you prepared for your next amazing opportunity.

19

Level Up Your Career

"It starts by believing in you."
—Jeannette Seibly

I remember lamenting years ago about a struggle I was experiencing in my business. I asked a coach, "Why?"

Her response was something I've not forgotten. "First, you have to believe in yourself."

I would add, "Then, you have to be willing to share your value and worthiness in a way that supports that belief in you!" (Hint: *Get Your Brag On!*)

Stepping up will feel uncomfortable at first. The biggest issue I've found with clients is when they tell themselves, "I have it all handled." They are being uncoachable. Then, it's only a matter of time before they are let go from their new position or opportunity.

It's critical to hire an executive coach and work with an industry mentor and be coachable to work through sticky situations and political relationships! Remember, take these new experiences one moment at a time, one day at a time, until it becomes your new normal. Again, be coachable (I cannot say that enough).

Do. Not. Let. Others' Opinions. Stop. You!

- Being vulnerable and stepping outside your comfort zone will invoke fear about what others will think. You may have fears that others won't like you, will mimic you, or ridicule you. Instead, think, they may applaud you and appreciate you for finally owning your accomplishments and sharing your successes in a business-savvy manner!

- Do not let naysayers get in your way. Or, it may be time for a new employer, clients, co-workers, or friends.

- Continue to embrace your achievements by updating and sharing your achievements as you accomplish new successes, and share them.

- Stay present when conversing with others.

- Success is an inside job. What goes on inside of you is a reflection of your feelings, thoughts, and opinions about you, and is shown on the outside no matter how carefully you try to hide things. Develop a healthy self-image and strong inner power.

- Owning your accomplishments and sharing them in a way that sells you is a great way to move forward in your career and life and create new unlimited choices that seemed previously unavailable.

- Remember, the next level in your development will not look the same as your current level. Hire a coach, find a mentor, and gather together friends for a mastermind group to support you! And, you, them!

- Believe in your accomplishments and share them. It shows others that you value yourself, and you value them too.

Examples of Leveling Up:

- Being a manager after having been an employee. This is a big step up. Remember, the successes that got you the promotion won't make the transition easier if you're not willing to be open to learning the next level up in a company. Or, going from employee to entrepreneur or solopreneur. Many practices are unwritten and go unnoticed until you fail to do or speak in what others consider to be an appropriate manner. Be coachable! You will discover there are many nuances at this new level—that's why it's crucial to have an experienced executive coach and industry mentor.

- You will experience new challenges, situations, and relationships when you change jobs—even if it's in the same profession or company. Have an external executive coach and an internal industry mentor to guide you through the "new hire" process. Meet regularly and listen! This is the key to growing and succeeding.

- Becoming a financially successful author is an attitude. Financial riches are a dream come true for only a few authors. Hire the right coach and do the work. Writing the book is only 10 percent of the process. The other 90 percent is the marketing, whether or not you work as an independent publisher or a publisher has bought your book. You still have to market and sell your book! Learn from professionals.

- When one of your ideas wins the company a new client or saves them millions of dollars, share it with your boss in writing and include it in your performance review. Also, use your brags when asking for or negotiating for a promotion, pay increase, or new opportunity.

Remember, life is more fun and rewarding when you love and honor you!

It starts with believing in you and sharing your brags! This is also the platform in which to create and pursue "what's next" in your career and life choices.

20

Mindfulness Keeps You Moving Forward

"It takes courage to do what you need to do for yourself.

It takes more courage to do it in a manner that leaves others inspired by your efforts."
—Jeannette Seibly

What is mindfulness? It refers to conscious awareness or presence. Improving this attribute will help you stay in business, win contracts, and have amazing conversations that lead to great business opportunities and positive recognition. It requires you to put down the phone and set aside your electronic gadgets to engage in conversations (including conversations on conferencing systems). These are very important to your success and require you to actively listen without thinking of other things during the conversation.

Unfortunately, as human beings, we take the tiniest fragments of information, nonverbal cues, or words and misinterpret them as well as personalize them. The ego takes over, and it's downhill from there. Being mindful is the best way to catch these actions or attitudes quickly and correct them even faster!

Being an entrepreneur, solopreneur, salesperson, consultant, author, business boss/leader, or business owner can be lonely, and will have its ups and downs. Resilience is key.

Staying positive and courageous when things are not going well can be a challenge, and too often, people will check out mentally or emotionally. They will allow others and their own self-talk to sabotage them. This is when developing and focusing on mindfulness and working through the issues and building intended results is critical.

The following are simple ways to remind yourself that you are a great person, develop positive self-talk, and continue to offer great products and/or services to others.

When you feel good about yourself, it naturally comes across in how you communicate—your energy—and your willingness to recognize yourself as a winner.

Brag!

On a daily, weekly, and/or monthly basis, write out your "I am …" and "My background includes …" statements. Review them and post them on your mirror. Rewrite them in your journal. Share them with others. This will help reinforce your achievements and you will exude natural confidence. When I journal, I write down at least three Brags.

The "I Am" Alphabet

Use the alphabet to create "I choose to be …" "I am …" or "I have …" statements. Have fun and enjoy coming up with one word for each letter of the alphabet to describe yourself.

Keep in mind there are many choices!

Start with: I choose to be … (Or, I am … Or, I have …) and go through the alphabet.

(Example: I choose to be joyful. (Or, I am joy. Or, I have joy.)

A = Assertive
B = Brilliant
C = Competent

These can be done first thing in the morning or before you fall asleep at night. Also, use them while you are driving to an appointment or when you have had a challenging day. Any time is the right time.

What Good Things Happened This Morning, This Afternoon, or Today?

You can answer this question at any time during the day, before you fall asleep at night, after a meeting, or on your way to your next meeting. If you journal, this is a great question to answer in addition to listing those things you are grateful for.

I include "Brags" from the previous day when journaling.
This is an important reminder to be aware of what
I'm doing and the results I'm producing.

Stay Fit Mentally, Physically, and Emotionally

Walk it out. Walk or run at least a mile per day or do any other type of aerobic exercise that you enjoy. Another fun way to keep your body moving is to use a pedometer. Set a target and achieve it each day.

Talk it out. Talk with a few selected and trusted coworkers or a boss when confronted with a challenge. Hire an executive coach or business advisor, even if you need to pay for it yourself. Talk to the clergy of your religion. Or, commit to seeing a licensed and trained professional on a consistent basis until you have resolved any personal or professional challenges. Keep in contact with others via social media venues as well as face to face! Stay involved in social activities. Refrain from engaging in "ain't it awful" sessions on social media, in networking groups, or when attending workshops or seminars. Remember, what you share can come back to haunt you!

Write it out. Keep a diary or journal. It's not for the benefit of others but for voicing your opportunities and challenges in writing. Studies show that writing things down can make a huge difference. Do not send hate letters or nasty emails, texts, or other types of messages when situations do not go your way or when you are upset. It could cost you your job, client, or opportunity.

Improve Your Results …
What Worked? / What Didn't Work?

This one will require you to write down your responses to receive the greatest benefit.

Too often, we are unaware of what is going well or specifically what needs to be fine-tuned to achieve our intended results. We create a blanket statement about the project or client being difficult, good, or great. It can ruin our day if we gloss over any details or issues that need to be addressed.

You can base this exercise on a project, customer, or sales process when things seem to be unworkable, or you have become over-whelmed. It's also good to complete daily, weekly, monthly, and annually and any other time period that is meaningful to you. Set aside 20 minutes and complete the following exercise.

What Worked? Start here—too often, we automatically go to the negative or the excuses. Using metrics, list all the things that are working. To get started, write down the key aspects of the job, project, or customer that have been working. For example, "XYZ customer loved the proposal since it saved them $xx." Yes, use your numbers!

What Did Not Work? Second, using your numbers (or metrics) list the things that specifically are not working. For example, "Missed my goal during Q1 to increase sales by yy percent." Stay away from excuses.

Review the First Two Categories. Don't forget to include anything else that is important to you, the project, your boss, your clients, the team, etc.

What Would You Like to Be Acknowledged For? Yes, human beings hate to be acknowledged! (Yes, even after having done their brag work.) Write down the achievements for which you would like to be acknowledged. Use short phrases, for example, "I increased attendance to 100 percent at team meetings." It really does feel good!

Keep Writing Even After You Believe You Are Finished. Again, don't forget to quantify your results or activities: "Improved xxx system by decreasing time spent by yyy percent." Consider using 2 numbers to help you clarify what you've achieved rather than simply stating, "I worked fewer hours on xyz."

You'll find it inspiring to see you've accomplished more than you originally thought. Then, update your KTAs for future brag statements.

Now, share this information with the "person in the mirror" if you do not have another person or small group to share it with. This process can be cathartic. It rids you of self-limiting conversations based upon excuses and "shoulds," and it's also a great team exercise for getting everyone on the same page. It refocuses you on specific actions to get you back on track while opening up conversations with others to handle missed results. It will naturally rejuvenate your personal satisfaction and professional commitment, and that of your team.

About the Author

Straight talk with dynamic results!

Jeannette Seibly has been an internationally recognized Talent Advisor and Leadership Results Coach for more than 32 years, with a total of 40+ years working with entrepreneurs, executives, and business owners. She has helped hundreds of companies use job fit technology to improve retention, hire the right person for the right job and team, and create strategies for high-impact results through coaching and consulting.

Her work with thousands of small business owners, family-owned businesses, sales professionals, business consultants, and boss/leaders makes a positive difference in helping them wow prospective clients and industry leaders faster. Along the way, three executives became millionaires, and Jeannette helped create more than 40 new executives.

Jeannette has earned the right to brag. Her savvy tips and techniques will show you how to create your own bragging rights during networking meetings and sales presentations, and by winning coveted industry recognition.

To learn more about Jeannette Seibly and her other products and services, contact her at https://SeibCo.com/contact/

How to Work with the Author

To learn more about Jeannette Seibly and her other products and services, contact her at https://SeibCo.com/contact/

"Straight talk with dynamic results"

Contact Jeannette for a complimentary conversation.

Jeannette provides the following services:

Leadership Results Coach – Achieves dynamic results working with business owners, executives, and key employees to hire, coach, and manage their people and achieve intended results.

Talent Advisor – Coaches and consults to design hiring, coaching, and managing practices that make a positive difference and uses qualified assessments for job fit.

Speaker – For keynote and workshop presentations.

KTAs

Knowledge	Talent	Achievements

KTAs

Knowledge	Talent	Achievements

KTAs

Knowledge	Talent	Achievements

www.ingramcontent.com/pod-product-compliance
Lightning Source LLC
Chambersburg PA
CBHW070719130626
46553CB00005B/2068